Giant Anaconda and Other Cryptids

FACT OR FICTION?

CREATURE SCENE INVESTIGATION

CREATURE SCENE INVESTIGATION

Giant Anaconda and Other Cryptids

FACT OR FICTION?

Rick Emmer

CHELSEA HOUSE
PUBLISHERS
An imprint of Infobase Publishing

GIANT ANACONDA AND OTHER CRYPTIDS: FACT OR FICTION?

Chelsea House
An imprint of Infobase Publishing
132 West 31st Street
New York NY 10001

Library of Congress Cataloging-in-Publication Data
Emmer, Rick.
  giant anaconda and other cryptids: fact or fiction? / by Rick Emmer.
    p. cm. — (Creature scene investigation)
  Includes bibliographical references and index.
  ISBN 978-0-7910-9782-3 (hardcover)
  1. Monsters—Juvenile literature. 2. Animals—Folklore—Juvenile literature. I. Title.
II. Series.
  QL89.E46 2010
  001.944—dc22   2009011460

Chelsea House books are available at special discounts when purchased in bulk quantities for businesses, associations, institutions, or sales promotions. Please call our Special Sales Department in New York at (212) 967-8800 or (800) 322-8755.

You can find Chelsea House on the World Wide Web at http://www.chelseahouse.com.

Text design by James Scotto-Lavino, Erik Lindstrom
Cover design by Takeshi Takahashi
Composition by EJB Publishing Services
Cover printed by Bang Printing, Brainerd, MN
Book printed and bound by Bang Printing, Brainerd, MN
Date Printed: April 2010
Printed in the United States of America

10 9 8 7 6 5 4 3 2 1

This book is printed on acid-free paper.

All links and Web addresses were checked and verified to be correct at the time of publication. Because of the dynamic nature of the Web, some addresses and links may have changed since publication and may no longer be valid.

CONTENTS

PREFACE

Welcome to Creature Scene Investigation: The Science of Cryptozoology, the series devoted to the science of **cryptozoology**. Bernard Heuvelmans, a French scientist, invented that word 50 years ago. It is a combination of the words *kryptos* (Greek for "hidden") and *zoology*, the scientific study of animals. So, cryptozoology is the study of "hidden" animals, or **cryptids**, which are animals that some people believe may exist, even though it is not yet proven.

Just how does a person prove that a particular cryptid exists? Dedicated cryptozoologists (the scientists who study cryptozoology) follow a long, two-step process as they search for cryptids. First, they gather as much information about their animal as they can. The most important sources of information are people who live near where the cryptid supposedly lives. These people are most familiar with the animal and the stories about it. So, for example, if cryptozoologists want to find out about the Loch Ness Monster, they must ask the people who live around Loch Ness, a lake in Scotland where the monster was sighted. If they want to learn about Bigfoot, they should talk to people who found its footprints or took its photo.

A cryptozoologist carefully examines all of this information. This is important because it helps the scientist identify and rule out some stories that might be mistakes or lies. The remaining information can then be used to produce a clear scientific description of the cryptid in question. It might even lead to solid proof that the cryptid exists.

Second, a cryptozoologist takes the results of his or her research and goes into the field to look for solid evidence that the cryptid really exists. The best possible evidence would be an actual **specimen**—maybe even a live one. Short of that, a combination of good videos, photographs, footprints, body parts (bones and teeth, for example), and other clues can make a strong case for a cryptid's existence.

In this way, the science of cryptozoology is a lot like forensics, the science made famous by all of those crime investigation shows on TV. The goal of forensics detectives is to use the evidence they find to catch a criminal. The goal of cryptozoologists is to catch a cryptid—or at least to find solid evidence that it really exists.

Some cryptids have become world-famous. The most famous ones of all are probably the legendary Loch Ness Monster of Scotland and the apelike Bigfoot of the United States. There are many other cryptids out there, too. At least, some people think so.

This series explores the legends and lore—the facts and the fiction—behind the most popular of all of the cryptids: the gigantic shark known as Megalodon, Kraken the monster squid, an African dinosaur called Mokele-mbembe, the Loch Ness Monster, and Bigfoot. This series also takes a look at some lesser-known but equally fascinating cryptids from around the world:

- the mysterious, blood-sucking Chupacabras, or "goat sucker," from the Caribbean, Mexico, and South America
- the Sucuriju, a giant anaconda snake from South America
- Megalania, the gigantic monitor lizard from Australia
- the Ropen and Kongamato, prehistoric flying reptiles from Africa and the island of New Guinea
- the thylacine, or Tasmanian wolf, from the island of Tasmania

- the Ri, a mermaidlike creature from the waters of New Guinea
- the thunderbird, a giant vulture from western North America

Some cryptids, such as dinosaurs like Mokele-mbembe, are animals already known to science. These animals are thought to have become extinct. Some people, however, believe that these animals are still alive in lands that are difficult for most humans to reach. Other cryptids, such as the giant anaconda snake, are simply unusually large (or, in some cases, unusually small) versions of modern animals. And yet other cryptids, such as the Chupacabras, appear to be animals right out of a science fiction movie, totally unlike anything known to modern science.

As cryptozoologists search for these unusual animals, they keep in mind a couple of slogans. The first is, "If it sounds too good to be true, it probably isn't true." The second is, "Absence of proof is not proof of absence." The meaning of these slogans will become clear as you observe how crypto-zoologists analyze and interpret the evidence they gather in their search for these awesome animals.

GIANT ANACONDA: SUPER-SIZED SNAKE FROM THE AMAZON

The study of mysterious, hidden animals is one of the newest life sciences, and certainly one of the most exciting.

—Loren Coleman, in Mark A. Hall's,
Thunderbirds: America's Living Legends of Giant Birds

*T*here's no doubt about it, cryptozoology is an exciting science. Just imagine the thrill of being the first person to catch a glimpse of an animal that most people believed could not possibly exist. Perhaps this creature was thought to be a product of the human imagination, living only in ancient myths and legends. Perhaps it was an animal previously known only from **fossil** remains that were millions of years old. Perhaps it was a gigantic version of some known animal, twice the size of the largest specimen anyone else had ever seen.

Many such "impossible" creatures have been discovered over the years. Africa's awesome mountain gorilla and the fearsome Komodo dragon of Indonesia, for example, are animals that were once considered too fantastic to be real. It wasn't until actual specimens were collected and put on display that the public was convinced that these animals do exist.

Perhaps the most unlikely of all hidden animals was the Kraken, or giant squid. Before 1854, scientists believed that such monsters lived only in the mind, not in the deep waters of the ocean. But, in that year, the Danish scientist Japetus Steenstrup proved that these gigantic, nightmarish relatives of the octopus actually exist.

For every cryptid that has been discovered, dozens more remain hidden. It is the job of cryptozoologists to search for these unknown animals and determine whether or not they exist. This volume in the Creature Scene Investigation series takes a look at some of the more unusual cryptids that cryptozoologists have pursued over the years. Some of these beasts live on land, some swim in the sea, some fly through the air—and some, such as a 50-foot-long (15.2-meter) serpent we'll examine first, slither through the jungles and swamps of tropical rain forests.

Until an actual specimen of the Komodo dragon was obtained in 1912, few people believed any of the stories they had heard about the monstrous lizard from Indonesia. Today, the animal has become a popular attraction at zoos worldwide.

SUCURIJU GIGANTE: THE GIANT ANACONDA

In January 2008, newspapers carried a story about a Brazilian girl who was nearly killed and eaten by an **anaconda**, a huge snake that lives in tropical South America. (Anacondas are relatives of the smaller boa constrictor, which are often kept as a pet by snake fanciers.) According to the news story, the snake had grabbed the 7-year-old girl, coiled itself around her legs, and started to drag her into the jungle. Fortunately, her screams brought a machete-waving man running to her rescue. This brave fellow used his large knife to chop off the snake's head, saving the girl from an agonizing death in the slowly tightening coils of the huge reptile.

Later, the animal was weighed and measured. It tipped the scales at 440 pounds (200 kilograms) and was 30 feet (9.1 m) long. As big as it was, however, people weren't terribly surprised by its size. The anaconda has a reputation for being big. In fact, it's one of the longest snakes in the world, rivaling the giant **pythons** of Africa, Asia, and Australia. Because it is a lot bulkier than the more slender pythons, the anaconda is undoubtedly the world's heaviest snake.

No one knows just how big the anaconda can grow. Many people claim to have seen anacondas more than 30 feet (9.1 m) long. Actual measurements, however, have been made on only a few of these monsters. The longest one was reported to be 37.7 feet (11.5 m) long. Because this measurement is so much greater than all of the others, many **herpetologists** (scientists who study amphibians and reptiles) doubt its accuracy. Most snake experts believe the maximum length for the anaconda is slightly more than 30 feet. If they are correct, then the anaconda that attacked the girl in Brazil was one of the biggest snakes ever seen by humans. But it wasn't even close to being the biggest one that has ever been reported.

Many inhabitants of the Amazon rain forest say that an even bigger snake lives in the depths of the jungle. They call it *Sucuriju Gigante*, meaning "giant anaconda" or "giant boa," and they claim it can reach a length of 50 feet (15.2 m) or more. Many cryptozoologists believe that if the Sucuriju exists, it is probably just an unusually large variety of anaconda. Others think that it might be an as yet unknown species.

The scientific **genus** name for the anaconda is *Eunectes*. This snake is found in tropical regions of South America east of the Andes Mountains. It's also found on Trinidad, an island just off the coast of Venezuela. Although it is sometimes encountered on dry land, the anaconda prefers

Let's Get Technical: Scientific Names

Scientists give official two-part names to each kind of animal. The first part is the genus name, and the second part is the **species** name. A species is what we normally recognize as a particular kind of animal, such as the anaconda or the boa constrictor. All animals in the same species have similar traits. Scientists place closely related species in the same genus. For example, there are four species of anaconda; all of them belong to the genus *Eunectes*.

If two different species belong to the same genus, they are given different species names. That way, every species has a unique two-part name, and there is no confusion as to the identity of the animal. For example, *Eunectes murinus* refers to the largest species of anaconda, nicknamed the green anaconda. *Eunectes notaeus* refers to a different, slightly smaller species known as the yellow anaconda.

This two-part naming system (officially known as **binomial nomenclature**) avoids the confusion that can result when nicknames are used. For example, the green anaconda is also called the "water boa." A person who did not know that both of these names refer to *Eunectes murinus* might incorrectly assume that the green anaconda and water boa are different species.

living in or near swamps and slow-moving streams. (*Eunectes* means "good swimmer" in Greek.) Anacondas sometimes climb onto tree branches that overhang the water, where they can bask in the heat of the tropical sun.

The massive green anaconda gets its name from the olive-green background color of its back and sides. Black spots and blotches on top of the green background provide camouflage. This coloring makes the snake nearly invisible when it lies motionless among plants and shadows in or near the murky water, enabling it to hide from its enemies.

The green anaconda from South America can reach 30 feet (9.1 m) in length and weigh up to 440 pounds (200 kg). In this photograph, soldiers from Brazil hold up a 17-foot-long (5.2-m) green anaconda.

It also allows the snake to ambush fleet-footed prey that come within striking range of the snake's tooth-studded jaws.

Because the anaconda is not **venomous** like a cobra or rattlesnake, its bite does not inject deadly venom into its prey. The purpose of the bite is to hang on to the prey while the anaconda coils its body around the animal. An anaconda is a **constrictor**: It kills its prey by slowly tightening its coiled body around the helpless animal. The snake's viselike grip eventually becomes so tight that the animal stops breathing, its heart stops beating, and it dies.

Anacondas eat a variety of animals, including mammals (rodents, deer, pigs), birds (especially waterfowl such as ducks), reptiles (crocodiles and turtles), and fish (big catfish in particular).

Snakes have extremely flexible jaws and a very stretchy throat. As a result, they can swallow prey considerably larger than their own head. There is, however, an upper limit for prey size. Even a big green anaconda has trouble swallowing an animal that weighs much more than 100 pounds (45.5 kg). The 30-foot (9.1-m) anaconda that attacked that Brazilian girl would surely have swallowed her if she hadn't been rescued. But a grown man would be far too big and broad-shouldered to be eaten by a snake of that size. Yet, if some reports can be believed, the Amazon rain forest is home to some absolutely immense anacondas—snakes large enough to make a meal out of the biggest professional football player and still have room for dessert.

Man Versus Sucuriju

In 1907, British army officer Percy Fawcett was sent to the Amazon rain forest to settle a boundary dispute involving the countries of Bolivia, Brazil, and Peru. While exploring the land bordering these three countries, Fawcett encountered a resident who claimed to have killed an anaconda 58 feet (17.7 m) long. At first, the level-headed soldier didn't take this fellow's story very seriously. He assumed the man was just bragging. A few months later, however, Fawcett would change his mind.

According to Fawcett's report, he and his crew were slowly making their way up a remote jungle river in a dugout canoe. Suddenly, they were startled by the sight of the huge head of a monstrous snake passing beneath their boat. The snake swam ashore and started to make its way up the riverbank. Fawcett saw that it was a gigantic anaconda. He quickly grabbed his

In 1907, British army officer Percy Fawcett claimed to have shot a *sucuriju gigante*, or giant anaconda, that was 62 feet (19 m) long.

rifle, "and hardly waiting to aim, smashed a .44 soft-nosed bullet into its spine, ten feet below the wicked head."

Fawcett ordered his terrified crew to paddle ashore so they could get a close look at the beast. As best he could guess—because part of the snake's tail was in the water and out of reach—the anaconda was an amazing 62 feet (19 m) long. To obtain evidence to back up his story, Fawcett tried to cut off a piece of the snake's skin; but the injured animal was still alive and wiggling. Fawcett was unable to approach close enough to slice off a skin sample.

Several other stories of run-ins with giant anacondas have surfaced since Percy Fawcett's story was told. Still, herpetologists John Murphy and Robert Henderson, authors of the book *Tales of Giant Snakes: A Historical Natural History of Anacondas and Pythons*, are doubtful. They believe the details of these later stories suggest that they are simply knockoffs of Fawcett's original tale, using different names, dates, and places.

In 1948, however, a Brazilian newspaper printed an entirely unrelated story about an absolutely huge snake that had been killed along the edge of the Amazon River, near the city of Manaos. The snake was reportedly 131 feet (39.9 m) long and 31.5 inches (0.8 m) in diameter, and it weighed 5 tons (4,545.5 kg). What made this Sucuriju story stand out above all the rest was the fact that it included a photo of the dead snake on the beach.

Tim Dinsdale, an English cryptozoologist who spent many years searching for Scotland's Loch Ness Monster, was fascinated by this photo. After carefully analyzing the photo in his book *Monster Hunt*, Dinsdale decided that the photograph was not a hoax. That could only mean one thing: The monstrous Sucuriju in the photo must be real.

Details, Details

Dinsdale's opinion that the giant snake in the newspaper photo was real was based on a detailed study of its **anatomy**. He thought every visible feature of the specimen was so precise and realistic that it couldn't possibly have been faked.

However, certain features of the snake were unlike those of an anaconda. For example, its bulging eyes and "great bag of a mouth" were too big. Also, the snake was fattest at the sixth convolution, or looped coil, of its long body. Dinsdale believed this was significant because big constricting snakes were thought to be fattest at the fourth convolution. Considering all of the evidence, Dinsdale concluded that the snake must be an unknown species "of hugely greater dimensions than any known snake."

Unfortunately, Dinsdale's analysis was flawed. An engineer by training, he wasn't well educated in the science of herpetology. Some of his assumptions were wrong. In *Tales of Giant Snakes,* Murphy and Henderson note that the oversized eyes and mouth of the snake in the photo are simply swollen with gas. The gas was likely produced by **bacteria** that were **decomposing** the flesh of the dead animal's head. (The same effect can be seen in a dead, **bloated** fish floating in the water. The body of the fish is puffed up and its eyes may be so swollen that they look like they're ready to pop out of its head.)

The evidence about the sixth convolution of the snake's body is totally useless. Snakes don't have a specific number of convolutions in their body. (In fact, scientists don't even use the term *convolution* to describe any part of a snake's anatomy.) As it moves along the ground and around objects, a snake's body may have anywhere from zero to several loops. The bulge in the snake's body part that Dinsdale identified as the sixth convolution may have been bloated from gas produced by the decomposition of the partially digested remains of the snake's last meal. Unimpressed by Dinsdale's analysis, Murphy and Henderson conclude, "This so-called supersnake is clearly an anaconda, *Eunectes murinus.*"

Percy Fawcett's eyewitness account of the Sucuriju he killed has a couple of shortcomings as well. For one thing, the fact that he saw the snake swimming under the boat indicates that the incident occurred during the daytime. That's a bit odd, because anacondas are **nocturnal** animals. One wouldn't expect to see an anaconda crossing a river in the middle of the day. That alone, however, is not enough

LET'S GET TECHNICAL: TRICK PHOTOGRAPHY

Curiously, when Tim Dinsdale presented his analysis of the Sucuriju photo in *Monster Hunt,* he didn't include the actual newspaper photograph. Instead, he included a very detailed and accurate drawing of the dead snake. Dinsdale did not draw any other objects that were in the photo. He thought they were too blurry to be of any value in determining the size of the snake.

Among those blurry objects in the photo are a couple of people in the background. They are out of focus because they are standing so far behind the snake. They do, however, provide some sense of **scale**, or relative size compared to the snake. They also help to show that the snake is not the 131-foot (39.9 m) monster it is claimed to be. Any object (in this case, the snake) that is photographed very close to a camera's lens can be made to look much larger than objects (the people) that are much further away. Since the news story claimed the animal was 131 feet long, the photographer was attempting to use a bit of "trick photography" to make the snake look as big as possible.

reason to doubt Fawcett's story. Perhaps the animal had been disturbed where it was sleeping and was simply moving to a quieter place to rest.

Harder to accept is the fact that Fawcett did not get the snakeskin sample that he wanted. His story suggests he was quite a good marksman. According to Fawcett, he effortlessly shot a moving snake in the neck while he was perched in an unsteady canoe. With such skill, he could easily have shot the wounded animal again after he came ashore. One bullet to the head would have put the snake out of its misery. After that, it would have been easy to obtain that piece of skin— or the snake's entire skull. These items would have provided the evidence necessary to back up Fawcett's story. The fact that he didn't do this casts doubt over the whole incident. Without solid evidence to **corroborate**, or back up, an eye-witness account, cryptozoologists can only view a story such as Fawcett's as just that—a story.

Where's the Evidence?

There is no doubt that people have encountered huge anacon-das in the wilds of the Amazon rain forest. Witnesses may honestly believe that the snake they saw was 50 or 60 feet long (15.2 or 18.3 m). It is very difficult, however, to estimate the length of any snake unless it is stretched out straight. Most people overestimate the length of the snakes they see, whether it is coiled in a ball or zigzagging through a mucky swamp.

The American adventurer Hyatt Verrill proved this point one day while exploring a river in the country of Guyana with some friends. Verrill spotted a large anaconda coiled on a rock beside the river. He asked each of his companions to guess how long the snake was. One man, who had never been in the rain forest before, guessed 60 feet (18.3 m) long. Another fellow, who had experience as a snake-collector, guessed 30 feet (9.1 m). The guesses of the other members of the group ranged from 20 to 40 feet (6.1 to 12.2 m).

After everyone finished guessing, Verrill shot the ana-conda, stretched it out, and measured it. It was only 19.5 feet (5.9 m) long. Everyone had overestimated the snake's length. Only one guess was reasonably accurate.

These results may explain why so many giant anacondas have been reported over the years. People may estimate the big snake to be two or three times longer than it really is. As a result, a 20-foot green anaconda morphs into a 40- to 60-foot-long (12.2- or 18.3-m) *Sucuriju Gigante*.

Even if someone were to submit as evidence a super-sized snakeskin, it wouldn't prove that the Sucuriju exists.

This is because a snake skin stretches a lot when it is removed from a dead snake. To prove this, one herpetologist carefully skinned a 24.5-foot-long (7.5-m) anaconda, while stretching the skin as little as possible. When he was finished, the skin could be stretched out to a total length of 34.5 feet (10.5 m).

It's possible, in fact, to stretch a snakeskin by as much as 50%. This means that the skin of a 30-foot-long (9.1-m) anaconda could be stretched to a length of 45 feet (13.7 m). That's a respectable size for any Sucuriju.

TITANOBOA

For many years, scientists believed that 30 feet (9.1 m) was the maximum length any snake could grow. That was the maximum observed in modern-day anacondas and pythons, and it was the maximum found in the largest known fossil snake, an extinct African species of the genus *Gigantophis*. No one knew for sure what was so significant about this length. Perhaps big, bulky constrictors longer than 30 feet had a hard time finding good hiding places. Or perhaps they were unable to find enough suitable-sized prey to keep from starving.

Then, in February of 2009, scientists made a remarkable discovery. While researcher Jason Head and his team of **paleontologists** were digging up 60-million-year-old fossils from an ancient rain forest in the South American country of Colombia, they discovered many huge fossil **vertebrae** from several specimens of an unknown species of snake. The structure of the vertebrae indicated that this new species was related to today's anacondas and boa constrictors, so the scientists gave it the genus name *Titanoboa*, which is Greek for "giant boa." By comparing *Titanoboa* vertebrae with vertebrae of anacondas of known size, Head calculated that these monstrous snakes measured up to 42.6 feet long (13 m) and weighed up to 2,497 pounds (1,135 kg). So much for the "30-foot maximum" rule!

Unfortunately, this exciting discovery does not mean that snakes of this size might still exist in the South American rain forest. According to Head, **poikilothermic** ("cold-blooded") animals like snakes grow larger at higher temperatures. He has suggested that *Titanoboa* was able to grow as large as it did because the South American rain forest was much warmer 60 million years ago than it is today. Research by other scientists indicates that the ancient Colombian rain forest had an average annual temperature somewhere between 86° and 93.2°F (30°-34°C), compared to the current annual average of only 80°F (27°C). If Head is right, then *Titanoboa* would not be able to grow so big in the cooler present-day rain forest.

All may not be lost, however. Many scientists believe that our planet is heating up once again, through a process called **global warming**. If Earth eventually becomes as warm as it was 60 million years ago, then anacondas might some day grow as large as *Titanoboa* did. If they do, then the *Sucuriju Gigante* will not remain an unknown animal for long.

CHUPACABRAS: BLOODSUCKER FROM PUERTO RICO

*I*n the 1970s, the Puerto Rican town of Moca was terrorized by an unknown creature that savagely killed many pets and farm animals. In each instance, the dead animals appeared to have been drained of blood from two holes poked in the neck. For obvious reasons, this monster was named the "Vampire of Moca." No one ever identified the blood-sucking beast and, after a while, things settled down. Over time, the incident was largely forgotten.

Then, in March 1995, the town of Orocovis experienced the first of another string of animal **mutilations**. As before, animals appeared to have been totally drained of blood and had puncture wounds in or near the neck. The first attack resulted in the deaths of eight sheep. Later attacks claimed the lives of different types of animals, including many goats. One day, a local TV personality jokingly referred to the animal killer as *el Chupacabras*. The term is Spanish for "the Goatsucker." It was then that the animal mutilator became an instant celebrity.

It quickly became clear that there was more than one Chupacabras. Although the first few goatsucker sightings centered on Orocovis, stories soon poured in from all over Puerto Rico. Some of these sightings were incredibly bizarre. In one case, a police officer who was investigating the mutilation of a farmer's sheep noticed a strange creature hiding in the shadows. The creature was **humanoid** in appearance, about 3 feet (1 m) tall, and had orange eyes. The officer tried to chase the creature, but it produced a foul odor that made the man so sick that he had to give up the chase.

In another incident, a man noticed a strange animal perched in a tree. This creature had a round head, black eyes, and a tiny mouth. Its skin kept changing color from brown to purple to yellow. It waved its head back and forth, producing a hissing noise that made the witness feel faint. Then it jumped to the ground and ran away.

Chupacabras sometimes take to the air. According to one report, some sort of winged monster attacked an elderly man who was working in a sugarcane field. The terrified man had a heart attack and died. In another case, a man saw a 5-foot-tall (1.5-m) creature that had big, slanted eyes and fins down its back. It produced a buzzing noise as it flew by wiggling its fins back and forth. The creature landed briefly in the man's yard, then jumped into the air and flew away.

In addition to these strange accounts, people noticed that some Chupacabras sightings occurred at the same time as UFO (unidentified flying object) sightings. UFO sightings are common in Puerto Rico. These paired sightings led many people to believe that Chupacabras might be aliens from outer space.

WILL THE REAL CHUPACABRAS PLEASE STAND UP?

The year 1995 was a good one for Chupacabras sightings. Many residents of farm towns in Puerto Rico claimed they saw goatsuckers that year. Investigations of these reports, however, became bogged down because eyewitness descriptions of the bloodsucker varied widely. The Chupacabras didn't seem to be one type of animal. Its size, color, and shape varied with each story. Sometimes it ran and sometimes it hopped. Sometimes it flew through the air, using either wings or flippers on its back, and sometimes it hovered motionless above the ground. In some accounts, it produced a sickening odor (variously described as smelling like battery acid, paint thinner, or sulfur fumes) that it used to paralyze its victims before it attacked. This same odor gave people headaches and made them sick, allowing the Chupacabras to escape from its pursuers.

Most Chupacabras descriptions, however, fall into one of two main categories:

(1) A big-toothed, big-eyed, doglike creature that can stand on its hind legs and jump like a kangaroo. Its skin is sometimes described as furry, but it is often reported as being hairless.

(2) A lizardlike creature with leathery green or gray skin. This animal has a row of spines down the middle of its back, similar to the crest that runs down the back of the iguana lizard. It also has fangs and

a forked tongue like some snakes, but its head looks more like that of a dog or cat. Its eyes glow red or orange when it's angry.

WHERE DID IT COME FROM?

The Chupacabras is undoubtedly the strangest of all cryptids. The varied accounts make it sound like a shape-shifting vampire straight out of a horror movie. Despite the different types of Chupacabras that have been described, however, most of them share one rather odd characteristic: Different parts of their bodies seem to come from different animals, such as snakes, lizards, dogs, cats, kangaroos, and bats.

An animal that has body parts like those of different kinds of animals is called a **chimera**, named after an imaginary monster from Greek mythology. This beast had the head of a lion, the body of a goat, and the tail of a snake. The Chupacabras certainly sounds like a modern-day chimera. Unlike the mythological chimera, however, the Chupacabras is believed to be real by many people.

Could such a beast actually exist? If so, where did it come from? Such a creation could only come from the mind of a mad scientist such as the one in H.G. Wells's classic novel *The Island of Dr. Moreau*. Dr. Moreau experimented on unwilling humans and animals to create hideous human-animal chimeras. One of these, a man-cat beast, finally escaped and killed the mad doctor.

Some people think that Chupacabras were created during experiments conducted in a secret government laboratory in Puerto Rico. According to this belief, scientists at this Dr. Moreau-like lab have discovered ways to join body parts of different animals to create real-life chimeras. Some of these chimeras are bloodthirsty Chupacabras that escaped from the lab and are roaming the Puerto Rican countryside, killing other animals.

The Chupacabras has been described by eyewitnesses as having features of both a dog and a lizard. It has primarily been sighted in Mexico and Puerto Rico. Despite the eyewitness accounts, scientists do not believe it really exists.

The chimera was a monster from ancient Greek mythology. It had the head of lion, the body of a goat, and the tail of a snake. Sometimes it was also said to have a goat's head sticking out of its back. The lizard-like form of Chupacabras is a modern-day chimera that is part lizard, part snake, and part dog.

One technique for creating these chimeras was supposedly perfected by Dr. Tsian Kanchen, a mysterious Chinese scientist living in Russia. An article in a Russian UFO magazine claimed that Kanchen discovered an unusual "bioelectromagnetic field" that exists in animal cells. This energy field somehow controls the growth of all of an animal's body parts. Normally, the body parts all belong to the same type of animal—say, a rabbit. Dr. Kanchen supposedly found a way to mix up the bioelectromagnetic fields of different species, allowing him to create rabbit-goat and chicken-duck chimeras. He even supposedly succeeded with plants, creating a sunflower-peanut.

Could Chupacabras really be chimeras that escaped from a secret government lab where experiments on bioelectromagnetic fields were being conducted? Most serious cryptozoologists don't think so. Considering the source of the Kanchen story, and knowing that the mysterious bioelectromagnetic field he supposedly discovered doesn't really exist, the only logical conclusion to draw is that the story in the UFO magazine is a hoax.

So, if the Chupacabras isn't a chimera, then what is it?

THE EVIDENCE SPEAKS FOR ITSELF

When scientists explore a mystery, they try to come up with simple explanations before they construct more far-out, complex ones. And the simpler explanations often turn out to be correct. Following this strategy, cryptozoologists have come up with several simple explanations for those varied Chupacabras sightings without relying on UFOs and weird animal experiments.

First, some Chupacabras stories are nothing more than hoaxes. For example, one man initially claimed to have been roughed up by a Chupacabras, but he later confessed that his bruises resulted from a fist fight. Plus, thanks to photo-editing computer programs and the Internet, phony goatsuckers have been hopping and flying all over cyberspace for years.

Second, there are cases of mistaken identity. The doglike types of Chupacabras have turned out to be just that—dogs— or the dog's **canine** cousin the coyote. These well-known animals can be misidentified if they suffer from a skin condition called **mange**. Severe cases of mange produce almost

Sightings of the doglike form of Chupacabras that is often reported in Mexico and the United States are often just mangy canines. Here, a woman holds a photograph of what she claims is a Chupacabras. The mysterious animal was found dead on her ranch.

complete loss of hair along with raw, scabby, wrinkly skin, and a foul odor.

A dog with a severe case of mange looks quite a bit different from a healthy, furry dog. A dog that has lost its hair looks much thinner than normal. Its skinny, naked tail looks like it belongs on a rat or lizard, not on a dog. Its head looks ugly, even scary, especially if it's covered with wrinkles and scabby sores. The unpleasant odor given off by a mangy dog would explain the stench that is often reported in Chupacabras sightings. Not surprisingly, the few

TECHNICALLY SPEAKING: CANINE MANGE

$\mathcal{M}$ange is an ugly, painful skin condition caused by **mites**, tiny **parasites** that live on an animal's skin. Like spiders, mites have eight legs and belong to the group of animals known as **arachnids**. There are many species of parasitic mite, and each species prefers to live on only one or a few closely related **host** species. Canine mange is caused by mites that live on dogs, coyotes, foxes, and other members of the dog family.

Canine mange mites live just under the surface of the skin. Symptoms of mange first appear on a dog's head, where the mites burrow into the skin, causing tiny sores. Pus seeps out of these sores and dries into scabs. Soon, the hair falls out and the skin itself becomes thick and wrinkled. The itchy scabs and burrowing mites irritate the dog's skin, so the dog scratches it.

Scratching spreads the mites to other patches of skin. If the dog is not treated with mite-killing chemicals, mange can spread over the whole body. As a result, a dog can lose almost all of its hair. In especially bad cases of mange, the sores become infected and produce a foul odor. The dog gradually becomes weak and **dehydrated**, and may eventually die.

supposed Chupacabras corpses examined by scientists have turned out to be nothing more than dogs or coyotes with mange.

Some dogs are naturally hairless. The Mexican hairless dog, or Xolo, is sometimes mistaken for the Chupacabras. This unusual breed of dog is rare in the United States, but is a common pet in Mexico. With hairless skin, the tail of a rat, and the ears of a bat, the Xolo is quite unusual in appearance. Anyone not acquainted with the breed might wonder if it is a dog at all.

In August 2009, **taxidermist** Jerry Ayer of Blanco, Texas, received the hairless carcass of an odd-looking doglike critter. The animal had eaten poisoned bait set out by a farmer to kill the creature that was raiding his hen house. Ayer didn't know for sure what the beast was, but he knew for sure what it wasn't: a Chupacabras. (Ayer doesn't believe in goatsuckers.) Except for its slightly longer-than-normal front legs, Ayer thought the skeleton looked just like that of a coyote— or perhaps a dog-coyote **hybrid**.

Despite Ayer's claim that the animal was just a canine, the news media had a field day with the incident. Stories about the chicken-killing Chupacabras from Texas popped up all over the place. For example, the *Los Angeles Times* online published an article titled "Is That a Chupacabra[s] Being Stuffed by a Taxidermist in Texas?" The article included two photos of the dead animal. Dozens of readers quickly responded to and even blogged about the article. The overwhelming majority—including a number of Xolo owners—immediately recognized the animal as a Xolo, not a Chupacabras. One blogger even criticized the *Times* for sensationalizing the poisoning of the poor dog.

Still, thanks to all the publicity, the story of the taxidermist's Chupacabras is now a popular new chapter in the legend of the goatsucker. Tissue samples from the animal were sent to scientists for precise identification, but their findings had not been announced by the time of this writing. If the animal turns out to be a mangy coyote/Xolo hybrid—a definite possibility—one might call it a coyolo or a Xolote, but definitely not a Chupacabras.

The lizardlike Chupacabras chimera can also be explained without resorting to UFOs or secret government experiments. Sometimes when people experience an extremely stressful or frightening event, their imaginations alter their perception. For example, on a dark night, a foul-smelling, furless, mangy dog may appear to be a monster. A single sighting of this beast can quickly spread by word of mouth throughout the community. Soon *everybody* is talking about it. Some people get so caught up in fear and excitement that they fool themselves into believing that a dark shadow they saw the night before must have been a similar creature. Only this one appeared to hop like a kangaroo, or flew away on bat wings. Before you know it, the legend of the Chupacabras, in all its varied forms, is born.

Such an emotional, chain-reaction-type response in a group of people is known as a **collective delusion**. History provides many examples of collective delusion, some of them silly, others pretty serious. One of the ugliest occurred in the 1690s in colonial Salem, Massachusetts, when a group of girls accused two women of being witches. To the highly religious residents of Salem, the thought that a neighbor might be a witch was cause for panic. Almost immediately, frantic people all over town began accusing one another of witchcraft. During the terrible Salem witch trials that soon followed, many innocent people were put in jail and tortured. At least 20 people were found guilty of practicing witchcraft and put to death. It took action by the governor of Massachusetts to put a stop to all the craziness.

Chupacabras sightings also have a lot in common with a condition known as **mass hysteria**. During mass hysteria, a group of people experiences similar symptoms of illness, even though there is no reason for them to be sick. The most common symptoms include upset stomach, headache, and dizziness. These are the exact symptoms experienced by many Chupacabras witnesses. The hysteria is usually triggered by something scary and/or a foul odor. Sightings of an unrecognizable, stinky, mangy dog wandering around in the dark of night would be a perfect trigger for mass hysteria.

A Couple More Details

Joe Nickell, a writer who has cast a **skeptical** eye on the Chupacabras craze, summarized his findings in his book *The Mystery Chronicles: More Real-Life X-Files*. He has made some interesting discoveries. For example, shortly after the Chupacabras became a worldwide celebrity, it began making guest appearances in other countries, especially Mexico. In one Mexican farming community where many farm animals were claimed to have been slaughtered by goatsuckers, police set animal traps to catch the culprits. They never caught a single Chupacabras, but they did catch several wild dogs.

Nickell also investigated the story of a Chupacabras that visited Florida, killing and draining the blood from a goat found near Miami—at least, that's the story that was reported. However, when a veterinarian examined the corpse, it was found that the blood had not really been drained from the body; it just looked that way. When animals die, blood that oozes out of open wounds often attracts flies and other insects. If the corpse lies around for a day or two before it is discovered, the insects drink much of that blood, making it look like the body has been "sucked dry." That is probably what happened in this case. Furthermore, the bite wounds on the animal indicated that it had been killed by a dog.

Whenever cryptozoologists gather enough evidence to identify a goatsucker, it turns out to be a mangy canine. When conditions are right, however, the human mind can transform that ugly, smelly, mite-infested animal into a monstrous, bloodsucking chimera. It is fortunate indeed that this hideous beast exists only in overactive imaginations. That means the creature won't ruin anyone's vacation in Puerto Rico, Mexico, Texas, or Florida. Nor will it escape from the laboratory of any mad scientist. And it certainly will never flutter down from the sky the next time a UFO pays Earth a visit.

Megalania and Tasmanian Wolf: Cryptids from the Land Down Under

So far, this Creature Scene Investigation has looked at two cool cryptids, the giant anaconda and the Chupacabras. No one has been able to prove that either of these beasts exists outside of the human imagination. The cryptids examined in this chapter, by comparison, are both known to have existed in the past. One is known only by its ancient fossil remains. The other survived well into the twentieth century before the last known specimen died. Both of these cryptids hail from the home of kangaroos, koala bears, and other famous **marsupials** (pouched mammals): Australia, the land Down Under.

Most scientists believe that these cryptids are extinct. Some cryptozoologists, however, believe that small, **relict** groups of both species may still survive. It is thought that they live in remote regions of the vast island continent of Australia. As is typical of most cryptozoological investigations, the evidence for the existence of either of these animals is sketchy at best. To hopeful cryptozoologists, however, even the slightest possibility that these animals survive makes the search for them worthwhile—and, as always, exciting.

MEGALANIA: THE MONSTER LIZARD

The **Aborigines** were the first people to inhabit Australia. When they set foot on Australian soil some 50,000 years ago, they were met by one of the most terrifying creatures imaginable—a huge dragon. Well, almost a dragon. The beast was actually a lizard and a close relative of Indonesia's famous Komodo dragon (*Varanus komodoensis*), or ora. Like the ora, this fearsome lizard, *Megalania prisca* by name, was a **ponderous** beast. It had massive, muscular legs that stuck out sideways in typical lizard fashion. This lord of the Australian **outback** roamed the countryside with a confident swagger.

If any animal deserved to swagger, it was *Megalania*. This huge lizard was the biggest **predator** of its time—at least twice the size of the 10-foot-long (3-m), 150-pound (68.2-kg) ora. *Megalania* had nothing to fear, and any animal it encountered was a potential meal. This monster was not a picky eater. It would consume anything it found, dead or alive. Swinging its head to and fro, it would sniff the air, hoping to pick up the aroma of its next lunch. It had an excellent

The giant Australian lizard *Megalania* preyed on large animals, including the ostrich-sized flightless bird, *Genyornis*.

sense of smell and could detect the scent of a rotting kangaroo carcass more than a mile (1.6 km) away.

Megalania was a crafty predator. It would hide in the bushes beside animal trails, waiting to ambush slow-pokes such as *Diprotodon*, a huge marsupial that resembled a gigantic guinea pig. All the big lizard had to do was jump out of the bushes and deliver one or two vicious bites with its sharp, **serrated** teeth. Even if the victim escaped, it would soon weaken and die, poisoned by venom produced by **glands** in the lizard's mouth. When the animal collapsed a few hours or days later, *Megalania* would track it down. The lizard would yank off huge chunks of meat and bone and gorge itself, eating half its own weight in a matter of minutes. When it had its fill, the big lizard would wander off to rest and digest its meal. It wouldn't need to eat again for months.

A Monster in Modern Times?

A scene like the one just described hasn't been witnessed by humans in quite a while. According to the fossil record, both *Diprotodon* and *Megalania* have been extinct for a long time. In *Megalania*'s case, it has been at least 19,000 years. Based on what herpetologists now know about the biology and hunting behavior of *Megalania*'s close cousin the ora, however, such scenes were common over the 4 million years that *Megalania* roamed the Australian outback.

Despite the fossil evidence, cryptozoologists have collected a handful of eyewitness accounts describing a *Megalania*-sized lizard. For example, while walking through a forest, two lumberjacks were once surprised by a huge lizard. The lizard lunged at the hand of one of the men and snipped off two of his fingers. The other lumberjack reacted quickly, driving a big spike into the lizard's head, killing the animal instantly. According to the report, the lizard was 20 feet (6.1 m) long. Unfortunately, a few days later, when people returned to the site of the attack, the lizard had vanished. With it went any evidence that it ever existed.

In another instance, a farm was visited by an unknown beast in the middle of the night. The farmer's dogs barked furiously. Then they tore after the animal as it wandered away. The dogs never returned. The next morning, the farmer discovered footprints of a huge lizard in the dirt near the chicken yard.

Australian cryptozoologist Rex Gilroy has been chasing after *Megalania* for many years. Gilroy made a plaster **cast** of a very large lizard's footprint found at another farm. The animal had apparently walked through a freshly plowed field.

A *Megalania* sighting was also reported on New Guinea, a large island located off the northern coast of Australia. There, a Catholic missionary claimed he once saw a gigantic lizard sunning itself on a fallen tree trunk.

In his book, *Dragons in the Dust*, *Megalania* expert Ralph Molnar points out that it's only *after* 1859 that the first monster lizard sightings were reported. That was also the year that the first *Megalania* fossil was discovered. This would suggest that people's imaginations got a little carried away with the discovery of the giant lizard's fossil remains.

It's important to note that another very large species of lizard still roams the Australian outback. In fact, it's *Megalania's* closest living relative. Called the perentie (*Varanus giganteus*), it grows to a length of 8 feet (2.4 m). As Hyatt Verrill's anaconda experiment suggested, people can overestimate the size of a snake by two or three times. So it's entirely possible that they could also overestimate the size of this snake-necked, whip-tailed lizard. Such errors could result in sightings of a *Megalania*-sized perentie 16 to 24 feet (4.9 to 7.3 m) long.

As far as those big-lizard footprints are concerned, cryptozoologists know only too well that such evidence can be a hoax. Thus, a cast of a big lizard footprint doesn't really prove anything. Until an actual specimen, dead or alive, is discovered, *Megalania* must stay in the ranks of unknown animals.

If *Megalania* were the top predator of the outback, with no enemies to worry about, why would it have become extinct? Before we answer this question, it's important to realize that *Megalania* wasn't the only giant roaming the land when the Aborigines arrived in Australia. All sorts of giant **herbivores** walked, hopped, burrowed, and lumbered across the landscape. These creatures included 440-pound (200-kg)

The perentie—a predatory lizard that grows up to 8 feet (2.4 m) long—is the most likely source of *Megalania* sightings.

kangaroos, giant flightless birds bigger than an ostrich, and *Diprotodon*, which grew as big as a rhinoceros.

These giant plant-eaters gradually became extinct between 50,000 and 20,000 years ago. If *Megalania* depended on the other giants for food, that would mean that as the herbivores died off, fewer big lizards could find enough food to survive. Eventually the last one would have starved to death, resulting in the extinction of its species.

There are two explanations for the extinction of Australia's giant animals. First, it's possible that Aborigine hunters killed them off. As the Aborigine **population** grew, more and more big animals may have been killed for food and clothing, until there were none left. Even if the Aborigines didn't hunt *Megalania*—a more dangerous foe would be hard to imagine—the Aborigines would have sealed its doom if they wiped out its food supply.

A second explanation is found in recent evidence collected by paleontologists. Their findings suggest that the extinction of the giants was more likely due to **climate change**. During the time period from 50,000 to 10,000 years ago, Earth experienced the most recent of many ice ages. During these periods, temperatures cooled down, glaciers in the mountains and at the North and South Poles grew larger, and many parts of the world, including Australia, became much drier. As a result, vast areas of moist, forested land that had provided food, water, and shelter for the giant herbivores turned into dry, open grasslands and deserts that could not support very many big animals. Conditions may have grown so severe that populations of these animals shrank to the point of no return, and the animals ultimately disappeared.

No one knows for sure which of these causes led to the extinction of Australia's huge herbivores. In fact, it's possible that Aborigines and climate change both played a part. In any case, the result would have been the same. Without enough food, predatory *Megalania* would have been driven to extinction.

A Glimmer of Hope

There is one recent discovery, however, that may offer a glimmer of hope to those searching for the long-lost lizard. In 2007, the zoo world was turned topsy-turvy when some eggs laid by an ora named Flora hatched at England's Chester Zoo. Female Komodo dragons in zoos had laid eggs before, so this in itself was no surprise. What made this event so newsworthy was the fact that Flora had never been kept with a male ora. She had never mated, and yet she had somehow managed to produce healthy eggs that hatched.

Other species of lizard are known to have accomplished this feat, but no one knew that Komodo dragons could do it. The process by which a female animal reproduces without breeding with a male is called **parthenogenesis**. This process works in different ways in different species. In some species, all the young produced by this process are female. In the ora, however, all the hatchlings are male. This is where the Komodo's cousin *Megalania* enters the picture. It is thought that if oras can reproduce by parthenogenesis, there's a good chance *Megalania* could do so as well.

Normally, when a population of animals becomes very small and spread out, males and females have a hard time finding mates for breeding. As a result, very few females produce offspring. Over time the population can become so small that no more offspring are produced, and the population dies out.

As the ice age wore on, the *Megalania* population undoubtedly shrank along with its shrinking food supply. At some point, the few remaining female lizards could find no mates. That problem might have been solved, however, through parthenogenesis. It would take at least a few years for males produced by parthenogenesis to reach breeding age, but if they survived and eventually found older females to breed with, the next generation would have both males and females. The females in this next generation could then reproduce via parthenogenesis, if necessary, producing another crop of males. This ability to shift back and forth between normal breeding and parthenogenesis just might have permitted *Megalania* to squeak by until food became more plentiful at the end of the ice age. It's a long shot, to be sure, but maybe it was just long enough.

THE TASMANIAN WOLF: THE MISUNDERSTOOD MARSUPIAL

After the disappearance of *Megalania*, a large marsupial became Australia's top predator. It was known by a variety of nicknames, including Tasmanian wolf, marsupial wolf, pouched wolf, Tasmanian tiger, and thylacine. Its scientific name is *Thylacinus cynocephalus*, which is Greek for "pouched thing with a dog head." The thylacine was a 70-pound (31.8-kg) meat-eater that looked like some sort of chimera. The female's pouch clearly showed that the animal was a marsupial, but it was shaped like a wolf and had tiger stripes down its back.

The thylacine was nowhere as big as *Megalania*, but it was still a fearsome predator. Its powerful, bulging jaw muscles made its head seem almost too big. It could open its sharp-toothed jaws far wider than any wolf or tiger—so wide, in fact, that it looked like the jaws were unhinged. After it ran down its prey, a thylacine could quickly clamp those massive jaws onto its victim's throat, dealing a suffocating, neck-breaking bite.

The fossil record indicates that the thylacine became extinct on the Australian mainland about 3,000 years ago. That is long before the first European settlers landed there.

The Tasmanian wolf was a powerful predator that sometimes preyed on farm animals, such as chickens and sheep.

Dingoes—small, **domesticated** wolves brought to Australia from Asia about 5,000 years ago—helped bring about their extinction. Aborigines and their dingoes were formidable competitors of the thylacine. They killed so many of the thylacine's prey that this marsupial predator eventually vanished from the Australian mainland.

Despite their disappearance on the mainland, as many as 5,000 thylacines still lived on the nearby island of Tasmania, where they were relatively free from human competition. Then, in 1803, the British landed there to establish a **penal colony**. Once the British established this foothold on the island, the fate of the Tasmanian wolf was sealed.

Tasmania was poorly suited for raising sheep. A group of wealthy businessmen, however, convinced British officials that northwestern Tasmania would be an ideal place to set up a sheep-farming business. If successful, the farm could support enough sheep to provide cheap wool for all of Britain. This would mean that the British would no longer have to buy expensive wool from other European countries.

In 1826, the Van Diemen's Land Company was established. Several huge parcels of land in northwestern Tasmania were set aside for sheep farming. During the first few years of the operation, thousands of sheep died from starvation and exposure to the cold, wet climate. Many other sheep were lost because of escapes through broken fences. Other losses were due to thefts by hungry seal hunters and penal colony inmates who worked as shepherds (sheep meat, or mutton, made a tasty meal). Occasional killings by wild animals such as eagles, **feral** dogs, and, of course, Tasmanian wolves accounted for still more sheep deaths.

The business owners were too proud to admit that the Van Diemen's sheep farm was a bad idea from the start and that the farm was poorly managed once it got going. So they looked for a **scapegoat** on which to place the blame. They found one: the Tasmanian wolf. Although thylacines did kill sheep from time to time, their contribution to the problem-plagued sheep-farming operation was minimal. Still, the thylacine was an easy target. It was, after all, a known predator of sheep—and a fearsome-looking one at that. Because people knew very little about the strange new animal in this strange new land, they were easily convinced that blood-thirsty thylacines were slaughtering herds of sheep.

As a result, **bounties** were paid to hunters who killed thylacines. The bounties were paid by the owners of sheep farms and by the government. Between 1830 and the early 1900s, several thousand Tasmanian wolves were killed. In

1909, the final year that bounties were offered, only two thylacines were shot.

The people of Tasmania and their government realized too late that this misunderstood marsupial was not to blame for the sheep industry's problems. By the time they learned this lesson, the animal was nearly extinct. Not that they hadn't been forewarned. As early as 1852, zoologist Ronald Gunn had predicted that the thylacine would become extinct if the killings continued at the same furious pace. On September 7, 1936, Gunn's prediction came to pass. The last known Tasmanian wolf died in captivity at a zoo in Hobart, the capital city of Tasmania.

Tasmanian Wolf Sightings

In the following years, thylacine sightings were reported from time to time, but nothing ever came of them. One well-known sighting in 1995 was particularly noteworthy as it was reported by a park ranger working in a wilderness area in northeastern Tasmania. The ranger claimed he had watched the animal for two minutes through his binoculars. He stated that he had clearly identified the animal by the tiger stripes on its back. Unfortunately, the story was later revealed as a hoax. A restaurant owner, in order to drum up business, had paid the ranger $500 to report his fake thylacine "sighting."

Another sighting is especially interesting, even though it proved to be a case of mistaken identity. This sighting took place on the Australian mainland in 1972. Robert Brown was a level-headed physician and a member of a group of cryptozoologists called the Thylacine Expedition Research Team. A skeptic by nature, Brown was almost certain that the thylacine was extinct. But he was fascinated by the animal and hoped to find evidence that would change his mind. One evening while driving home, Brown was surprised when he

Greyhounds with the brindle color pattern may be responsible for many thylicine sightings.

caught a brief glimpse of a striped animal that looked just like a thylacine. He immediately fetched another member of the research team and returned to the sighting location. Brown and his partner quickly tracked down the animal, only to find that it was a greyhound.

It's easy to understand Brown's mistake. Col Bailey, another thylacine chaser, describes the animal: "It's like a greyhound dog, very narrow in the **loins** but with a big deep chest which speaks of an animal that has a big endurance.

Let's Get Technical: Cloning

To produce a clone, or exact copy of one animal, **DNA** (deoxyribonucleic acid, the substance that genes are made of) is taken from one of the animal's body cells (for example, a muscle cell). This DNA is used to replace DNA taken from an egg cell removed from a second animal. This "new" egg cell is then placed in the **uterus** of the second animal. That animal then serves as a **surrogate**, or substitute mother, for the baby animal that grows from the egg cell. The baby grows into a clone of the first animal, since that was the animal whose DNA was inserted in the egg cell.

Scientists working on the thylacine-cloning project are trying to obtain DNA from a muscle cell of a female thylacine pup. The young animal died in 1866 and was preserved in a jar of alcohol. If the pup's DNA is still in good shape, it will be transferred to an egg cell from a female Tasmanian devil (*Sarcophilus harrisii*). This animal is a marsupial relative of the thylacine. The Tasmanian devil will then serve as the surrogate mother. If the egg survives and grows, the devil will eventually give birth to a clone of the preserved thylacine pup. The procedure will then be repeated, using DNA from a preserved male pup.

If things go as planned, Tasmanian devils will someday give birth to enough male and female thylacine clones to produce a healthy breeding group. Then the thylacine clones can be set free to roam and reproduce in the wilderness once again.

And stripes of course." Greyhounds come in a variety of color patterns. One of the more popular patterns occurs only in greyhounds, great Danes, and a few other breeds of dog. Known as *brindle*, this color pattern consists of a brown background with black blotches, stripes, or wavy patterns along the dog's back. Brown's "thylacine" was one of these brindle-patterned greyhounds.

Greyhound racing is a popular sport in Australia. More than 60 greyhound racetracks are located there. Tasmania has one in Hobart. Who knows how many Tasmanian wolf sightings are actually sightings of greyhounds—either unleashed pets or racing dogs that have escaped or been abandoned by their owners because they are too slow to race? We are now certain of one such sighting, and there could be more.

One of the most convincing arguments against the survival of the thylacine comes from a rather strange observation. Among the countless animals that are hit and killed on the back roads of Tasmania every year, there are scores of Tasmanian devils, kangaroos, wallabies, wombats, and other marsupials. In more than 50 years, however, not one thylacine roadkill has been reported. This odd fact, as much as any other, suggests that the animal is indeed extinct.

Send in the Clones

In 1999, an amazing project was undertaken—an attempt was made to **clone** a thylacine. Other animals have been cloned before. The most famous was Dolly the sheep, who was born in 1996 and died in 2003. The thylacine cloning project began at the Australian Museum, under the leadership of the museum's director, Mike Archer. Unfortunately, Archer resigned from his position at the museum in 2004. Under new leadership, the museum terminated the costly project in early 2005. However, Archer announced a few months later that scientists at other research institutes were planning to resume the cloning project. If they eventually succeed, it will be the first time scientists have been able to bring an extinct animal species back to the world of the living.

Many scientists think that this incredibly difficult venture is bound to fail. They believe that the huge amount of money being spent on the cloning project should be used to preserve the thylacine's **habitat**, just in case a few of these animals still roam the ever-shrinking wilderness. Yet, even if the cloning project is a big success, people will probably continue to look for wild Tasmanian wolves. Copies, after all, are never as good as the original.

THUNDERBIRD: BIG BIRD OF THE SKY

Native American folklore is rich with stories about big, strong, dangerous animals. We are well acquainted with most of these animals, such as wolves, bears, and buffalo. The animals in some of these stories, however, are such fantastic creatures that we assume they could exist only in the mind of an imaginative storyteller. Perhaps the biggest and most powerful of all these imaginary creatures were the Thunderbirds, beings that were part bird and part spirit.

Thunderbirds lived in a big cloud high in the mountains. They had a nasty habit of transforming the white, puffy clouds of a peaceful sky into a life-threatening rainstorm. They could

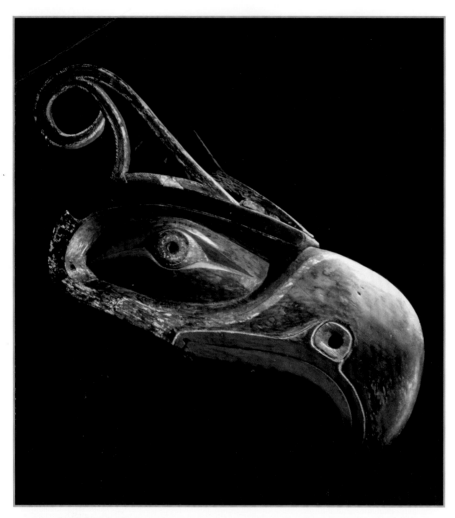

This Thunderbird headdress was carved by a Native American and used in ceremonial dances.

produce earthshaking blasts of thunder and crackling bolts of lightning just by flapping their wings and blinking their eyes. Sometimes they had a taste for human flesh.

One story told by the Winnebago tribe of the American Midwest is the legend of young Orphan-boy. One day long ago, Orphan-boy and a friend left their village to collect sticks to make into hunting arrows. Orphan-boy was so intent on his mission that he was caught off guard by a bad Thunderbird. The animal swooped down from the sky, snatched him up in its mighty hooked **talons**, and carried him to its cave high in the mountains. Orphan-boy was imprisoned there for many days while a flock of bad Thunderbirds prepared to eat him.

Fortunately, a little hawk that had befriended Orphan-boy found out what the bad Thunderbirds were up to. The hawk tattled on them to the good Chief Big Black Hawk, leader of the Thunderbirds. Upon hearing the little hawk's story, the chief became angry. He flew to the bad Thunderbirds' cave and freed Orphan-boy. When the boy recovered from his ordeal, the little hawk flew him back down the mountain and released him at the exact spot where he had been captured. Orphan-boy's friend, who had never stopped looking for him, soon found him. Reunited, the two boys returned to their village. Orphan-boy's safe return was celebrated with a feast of Thanksgiving.

An adventure such as Orphan-boy's could happen only in the land of make-believe, right? Well, if one modern-day family's story is true, then a boy from Illinois almost met the same fate as Orphan-boy.

ALMOST KIDNAPPED

According to the Lowe family of Lawndale, Illinois, little Marlon Lowe, a 65-pound (30-kg) 10-year-old, was almost snatched out of his backyard by a very big bird. One July evening in 1977, while young Marlon was playing outside with two friends, the boys saw two huge birds soaring in the sky. The birds then swooped down toward the boys, who fled in terror.

One of the birds grabbed Marlon by the straps of his sleeveless shirt and tried to carry him off. Marlon screamed and squirmed and punched at the bird as it lifted him 2 feet (0.6 m) off the ground. After carrying Marlon for a distance of 40 feet (12.2 m), it dropped him. Then both of the big birds flew down the street, toward a stand of tall trees bordering a creek. Despite his scary ordeal, Marlon was not injured. He wasn't even scratched by the bird's talons when they grabbed hold of his shirt.

Marlon's mother ran into the backyard when she heard him scream. She saw the bird drop Marlon to the ground and then fly away with its partner. Marlon's father and two other adults burst onto the scene just in time to see the birds as they flew away.

According to the witnesses, both birds were black, except for a ring of white feathers around the neck. They had wingspans of 8 to 10 feet (2.4 to 3.0 m) and were 4 feet (1.2 m) long from head to tail. Marlon's mother said that of all the birds she was familiar with, these two birds most resembled the California condor (*Gymnogyps californianus*), a huge vulture that lives in the far west and had never been spotted anywhere near the state of Illinois.

As soon as the Lowes' story became public, many additional sightings came flooding in. Cryptozoologists are only too aware of "copycat" sightings such as these, and take most of them with a grain of salt. One report, however, immediately grabbed the attention of scientists everywhere. Five days after Marlon was attacked, fisherman John Huffer saw two huge, black birds flying through the trees by Lake Shelbyville. The lake is 150 miles (240 km) southeast of Lawndale. Huffer always carried a movie camera with him. He used it to film the larger of the two birds as it flew through the nearby woods. According to Huffer, the bird had a wingspan of about 12 feet (3.7 m). He figured that these were probably the birds that visited Lawndale.

Weighing the Evidence

The Lawndale incident and the Huffer film are considered by many Thunderbird hunters to be the strongest evidence

Some cryptozoologists believe that turkey vultures are sometimes mistaken for the Thunderbird.

showing that some type of huge, unknown bird of prey lives in the American Midwest. Do these pieces of evidence deserve such high regard? The answer is both yes and no. Each story should be considered separately.

Fortunately for Marlon Lowe, the boy did not receive so much as a tiny scratch from the big bird's talons as they latched on to his shirt. This means, however, that Marlon had no scratches or scars to back up his story. Even his shirt escaped serious injury: It was only frayed a little, not torn or shredded when the big bird yanked him into the air. In addition, all of Marlon's punching and pounding failed to dislodge a single feather from the bird's legs or belly. For these reasons, the Lowes' story provides no more solid evidence for the existence of giant predatory birds than does the legend of Orphan-boy.

Huffer's film, however, is another matter. It clearly shows what looks like an enormous **raptor** flying through the woods by Lake Shelbyville. Wildlife experts who have studied the film say the huge bird just might be a big turkey vulture (*Cathartes aura*), a common vulture that has a wingspan of up to 6 feet (1.8 m). Despite difficult viewing conditions due to the shady woods, however, Huffer was certain that this bird was not a turkey vulture. That's because the bird didn't appear to have a red neck. A red neck, along with a red head, is characteristic of the turkey vulture.

To this day, Huffer's film is the best evidence yet for the existence of a gigantic bird of prey, a real Thunderbird. If Huffer was correct in claiming that the big bird he filmed was not an overgrown turkey vulture, just what type of bird could it be?

The Candidates

Based on the description provided by Mrs. Lowe and the appearance of the bird in Huffer's movie, it is clear that the bird in question is a large raptor. Mrs. Lowe thought the bird that attacked her son looked a lot like a California condor. So it makes sense to consider the condor and other vultures as Thunderbird candidates.

There are three species of vulture found in the United States. The condor, with a 10-foot-long (3-m) wingspan, is the only one that grows as big as the bird described by Huffer and the Lowes. The other two vultures are the turkey vulture and its gray-headed cousin, the black vulture (*Coragyps atratus*). Both birds are much smaller than the condor.

The black vulture has a wingspan of only 5 feet (1.5 m). Cryptozoologists, however, know well that people tend to exaggerate, sometimes greatly, the size of unknown animals that they encounter, so it's tempting to consider both of these smaller vultures as possible suspects, especially since they fit the general description of big, black birds of prey.

Unfortunately, there is a problem with vultures as candidates for the Thunderbird. Because they are scavengers that usually feed on **carrion**, or dead animals, vultures don't need powerful talons to kill their food. They eat their food where they find it on the ground. Therefore, they don't need strong feet to grab and hold onto prey as they fly to a safe feeding perch high in the trees. In fact, no vulture is strong enough to haul heavy prey into the air.

Eagles are another matter. These raptors have big, sturdy talons and strong feet that they use to kill their food and carry it up to a nest or perch in a tree. There are two species of eagle that are known to live in the United States. Both are almost as big as a condor, and both can hoist a fairly heavy animal into the air.

One eagle species is the bald eagle (*Haliaeetus leucocephalus*). It is highly unlikely that an adult bald eagle, with its trademark white head and tail feathers, could be mistaken for the mysterious Thunderbird. A young bald eagle's head and tail, however, are dark brown until the bird is three or four years old. By that age, the bird has reached adult size and sports a wingspan of up to 7.5 feet (2.3 m). Young bald eagles often sport a small patch of white or light gray feathers on their breast. This fact might explain the white feathers Mrs. Lowe claimed she saw on the neck of the bird that attacked her son. Finally, because fish are one of their favorite foods, bald eagles frequently live near streams and lakes. Both the Huffer and Lowe incidents occurred near water. Clearly, full-grown **immature** bald eagles should be considered as possible candidates for the Thunderbird.

Young bald eagles that have not yet grown their white head and tail feathers are powerful predators that may be mistaken for the Thunderbird.

The aggressive golden eagle with its 8-foot-long (2.4-m) wingspan is another likely candidate for Thunderbird sightings.

Another eagle species, even bigger and bolder than the bald eagle, should also be considered as a Thunderbird candidate. It is the golden eagle (*Aquila chrysaetos*). This magnificent soaring raptor can be found throughout the Northern Hemisphere. In North America, it is found from Canada to Mexico. It usually lives in remote, wild areas far from cities and towns. As a result, most people are not acquainted with this bird, and so they would be unable to identify a golden eagle on sight.

The golden eagle is dark brown in color, with lighter, golden-colored feathers on the back of the head and neck. It grows even bigger than the bald eagle. Females, which grow larger than males, can have a wingspan of nearly 8 feet (2.4 m). Golden eagles usually prey on animals weighing no more than 15 pounds (6.8 kg), but they have been reported to attack animals as large as adult deer. Clearly, the golden eagle must be considered as a possible candidate for the bird that attacked Marlon Lowe.

There is one more eagle species that must be mentioned in this investigation. It is said to grow even bigger than the golden eagle and, in its own way, is just as mysterious as the Thunderbird. It is named the Washington sea eagle. Famed American wildlife artist John James Audubon painted a portrait of this bird, which he claimed to have shot and killed by a river in the early 1800s. Audubon's bird was colored various shades of brown and had a wingspread of just over 10 feet (3 m). Audubon was convinced he had found a new species of bird. Scientists of his time, however, decided that the bird was simply a very large, young bald eagle that had not yet grown its white head and tail feathers. In any case, some hopeful cryptozoologists believe that the Thunderbird and Audubon's Washington sea eagle may be one and the same bird. If a Thunderbird is ever captured, we'll know for sure.

There is one other type of bird that has been connected to the Thunderbird mystery: the **teratorn**. Most scientists believe that this giant relative of vultures became extinct several thousand years ago. Some cryptozoologists, however, suspect that it still survives and may have been the bird that gave rise to the Native American legend of the Thunderbird.

Fossils of three species of teratorn have been discovered. Fossil bones of the smallest species, Merriam's teratorn (*Teratornis merriami*), have been found in the famous La Brea Tar Pits in California. This bird had a 14-foot-long (4.3-m) wingspan. The slightly larger incredible teratorn (*Teratornis incredibilis*), whose remains have been found in

The teratorn was a huge prehistoric vulture that may have given rise to the Native American legend of the Thunderbird. In this illustration, a teratorn battles a saber-toothed tiger over an animal carcass.

Nevada, had a wingspan of 17 feet (5.2 m). The largest teratorn, the magnificent teratorn (*Argentavis magnificens*), is known from fossils found in South America. This bird was indeed magnificent: It stood five feet (1.5 m) tall, had a wingspan of nearly 25 feet (7.6 m) and probably weighed more than 250 pounds (114 kg).

British cryptozoologist Karl Shuker believes that many modern-day Thunderbird sightings could easily be explained if one or more species of teratorn had managed to survive into modern times. Shuker points out, however, that Marlon Lowe's attacker could not possibly have been a teratorn. These birds, like their vulture cousins, had weak feet and talons. In fact, teratorn feet were even scrawnier than vulture feet. It's entirely possible that teratorns used their feet only for standing and walking, not for grabbing things. If Lowe really was attacked by a huge raptor, the culprit was most likely some sort of eagle.

LET'S GET TECHNICAL: FLYWAYS

Many birds migrate long distances every year. They fly between their food-rich spring and summer nesting areas up north and their warm winter homes down south. Dozens of raptor species migrate hundreds of miles back and forth, year after year. They always travel along the same narrow flyway—the bird equivalent of an interstate highway. The birds' routes are so predictable that some places have become popular vacation destinations for bird watchers.

One of the best places anywhere to watch migrating raptors is Hawk Mountain, in the Allegheny Mountains of Pennsylvania. During the 2007 autumn migration season, a total of 19,404 raptors of 20 different species were spotted winging their way south to their wintering grounds. Among those birds were 98 golden eagles, 140 black vultures, 230 bald eagles, and 636 turkey vultures.

Flyways often follow mountain ranges and coastlines, where rising air currents allow the big birds to soar long distances. Soaring means birds don't have to expend large amounts of energy by constantly flapping their wings. The Thunderbird flyways that cryptozoologist Mark Hall plotted from dozens of Thunderbird sightings match well with flyways used by eagles and vultures. Some people think that this is strong evidence that the huge birds really exist. However, it is possible that the Thunderbirds reported in these sightings are nothing more than misidentified migrating eagles and vultures.

A Pattern Emerges

Thunderbird hunter Mark Hall has made an interesting observation: When modern-day Thunderbird sightings are plotted on a map of the United States, a pattern emerges. The sightings seem to bunch up into three groups. These groups follow gently curving paths that flow in a more-or-less north to south direction for hundreds of miles. This suggests that Thunderbirds, like many birds, **migrate** along narrow **flyways** during the course of the year.

One flyway runs along the Pacific coast, from Alaska to California. A second flyway runs from Wisconsin down through Illinois and Missouri, and into the Ozark Mountains of Arkansas. The third flyway starts in eastern Canada, passes south into New York, cuts through Pennsylvania, continues into West Virginia and Kentucky, and ends in Tennessee. The timing of the sightings indicates that the birds migrate north in the spring and south in the fall. But if these huge birds follow migration routes, why aren't they seen all the time? Hall's answer is that Thunderbirds, like many other birds, prefer to migrate at night.

The Thunderbird is a puzzling animal. Much of the information gathered from sightings and encounters with these gigantic birds fits well with what is known about living and fossil raptors. Still, the mighty bird manages to avoid discovery by modern science. With the possible exception of the Huffer film, many scientists believe that all modern Thunderbird sightings are simply hoaxes or cases of mistaken identity, where eagles or vultures have been morphed into monstrous birds by excited, overactive imaginations.

To prove that the Thunderbird is a new species, Thunderbird hunters need to obtain an actual specimen. And that may be a pretty tall order—especially if the Thunderbird turns out to be a 250-pound (114-kg) relative of *Argentavis*, the magnificent teratorn.

Kongamato and Ropen: Return of the Pterosaurs

$\mathcal{T}$he discovery of a living *Megalania* or teratorn would certainly be an exciting event, since the fossil record indicates that these beasts became extinct thousands of years ago. Yet, think how much more exciting it would be if scientists discovered an animal that was supposed to have become extinct *millions* of years ago. Such an event happened in 1938, when a live **coelacanth** was caught by fishermen from the Comoros Islands in the Indian Ocean off the east coast of Africa. Because the coelacanth is a fish that was supposed to have gone extinct back in the days of the dinosaurs, catching a specimen was one of the most amazing scientific discoveries of the twentieth century.

Were another long-lost creature from that faraway time to be discovered today, it would undoubtedly be one of the most amazing discoveries of this century. If certain eyewitness reports are accurate, such an animal does indeed exist. But this animal doesn't swim in the ocean with the coelacanth. It soars through the air with vultures and eagles, and perhaps even with teratorns. It's not a bird, and it's not a bat. It's a reptile—a flying reptile. It's a **pterosaur**.

Many pterosaur sightings have been have been reported over the years. The examples that follow are just the tip of a very large iceberg.

NOT A BIRD OR A PLANE ... IT'S A KONGAMATO!

In 1923, the adventurer and explorer Frank Melland published a book about his adventures in Africa. One of his stories concerned a legend told by the Kaondé tribe of Zambia, a country in southern Africa. According to the Kaondé, fearsome, winged dragonlike creatures inhabited the vast, spooky Jiundu swamp. This was a dangerous place where few people dared to go—and those brave souls who did rarely returned to tell of their adventures.

These swamp beasts were called *Kongamato*, which means "boat breaker." According to legend, whenever a boat entered the territory of one of these monsters, the animal would swoop down from the sky, dive into the water, smash into the bottom of the boat, and tip it over. Everyone on board would be dumped into the snake-infested swamp. According to the Kaondé, the Kongamato was red in color and had leathery skin with no feathers, a tooth-filled beak, and a long tail. It had a wingspan of 4 to 7 feet (1.2 to 2.1 m).

This illustration is an artist's depiction of a prehistoric pterosaur. The Kongamato, or "boat breaker," is a pterosaur from Africa. It is said to attack people in or near the water, and reportedly smashes their boats to pieces. The ropen is a pterosaur from New Guinea and Australia. Like the Kongamato, it is known to attack people.

The Kongamato lived in other swamps as well. In 1925, a native was severely injured while exploring a swamp in Zimbabwe, a country just to the south of Zambia. The poor man, wounded in the chest, eventually escaped from the swamp and staggered back to his village. He claimed he was attacked by some sort of big bird that had a long, pointed beak. While the man rested in bed, someone gave him a picture book of prehistoric animals to see whether he could identify the strange bird that attacked him. The man flipped through the pages, looking at the pictures. When he turned to the page illustrating a pterosaur, the man screamed, jumped out of bed, and ran away. It was presumed he had been frightened by the sight of his attacker.

In 1956, an engineer named J.P.F. Brown reported seeing two pterosaurlike creatures flying by a river in the country of Zaire, Zambia's neighbor to the north. Each animal was fairly small with a doglike head, long toothy snout, and long tail. Each had a wingspan of only 3.5 feet (1.1 m).

Famous American cryptozoologist Roy Mackal spent several years searching for Scotland's Loch Ness Monster and the dinosaur Mokele-mbembe in the African Congo. In 1988, Mackal came to Namibia, just southwest of Zambia, to search for the Kongamato. Unfortunately, just as happened in his earlier expeditions, he never found his cryptid quarry. However, one of the expedition members, James Kosi, stayed behind after Mackal returned to the United States. Mackal had barely left Africa when Kosi reported seeing a huge, black-and-white pterosaurlike beast gliding high in the sky. Kosi estimated that the animal had a 30-foot-long (9.1-m) wingspan.

NOT A BIRD OR A PLANE ... IT'S A ROPEN!

Africa isn't the only place where people have seen prehistoric flying reptiles. Southeast Asia has had its share of sightings as well. Only here, the animal goes by a different name. It is called *Ropen*, or "demon flier." Reports of many Ropen sightings have come from the island of New Guinea. Most of these sightings report a winged creature with a wingspan of 4 feet (1.2 m), a long beak filled with tiny, sharp teeth, and a long tail. This nocturnal animal leaves its cave in the mountains at sunset to scavenge for carrion and to hunt for fish. Sometimes it tries to steal fish from fishermen's nets.

Among the many Ropen stories from New Guinea is a 1980s report of a farmer who was attacked and killed by a ropen as he worked in his garden. Another sighting occurred in 1994 when three young boys reported a monstrous Ropen with a 20-foot-long (6.1-m) wingspan and a very long tail flying near a lake. A 1995 report described an entire village watching a Ropen as it flew out to sea.

A giant Ropen known as a *Duah* also inhabits New Guinea. In addition to having at least a 20-foot-long (6.1-m) wingspan, this Ropen sports a bony head crest like the one found on *Pteranodon*, the famous giant pterosaur from North America. This monster is also a scavenger that has a nasty habit of digging up fresh graves to eat the bodies of people who were recently buried. The Duah also sometimes attacks living animals, including people. In 1944, an American soldier stationed in New Guinea spotted one of these animals as it took off from the ground and flew away. According to the soldier, the beast looked as big as the airplane he flew. His plane had a wingspan of 26 feet (7.9 m).

In Perth, a city along Australia's west coast, a husband and wife reported seeing a pterosaur flying overhead, 300 feet (91 m) in the air. The animal was reddish-tan with leathery, featherless skin on the wings, and fine, furry hair on its body. (One might wonder how the couple could see the fur clearly at such a distance. Even with the aid of binoculars, such a detail would be difficult to detect.) It also had a tail longer than its body and an impressive 30-foot-long (9.1-m) wingspan.

Living pterosaurs have been reported from many other places as well, including Europe and Japan. In the United States, sightings of *Pteranodon*, dubbed "Big Bird," have been reported many times. This nickname is a bit confusing, because many people use it when referring to the unrelated Thunderbird. That animal really *is* a big bird.

It's Practically Impossible

For a number of reasons, it's very unlikely that pterosaurs still exist. First, the fossil record indicates that the last flying reptiles died out with the last dinosaurs, 65 million years

Two completely different types of pterosaur soared in the skies in the days of the dinosaurs. One type had a long tail (*shown in this illustration*) and the other had a short tail. Reports of Kongamatos and Ropens have described both types of pterosaur, suggesting that both types still exist.

ago. If pterosaurs still exist, their fossil trail should lead right up to modern times. Second, if they still exist, surely someone would have collected a living or dead specimen by now. Third, the details of eyewitness descriptions of pterosaurs clearly suggest that two very different types of prehistoric flying lizard have survived to modern times, not just one. One is the short-tailed **pterodactyloid** and the other is the

LET'S GET TECHNICAL: PTEROSAURS

The pterosaurs ("winged lizards") were a truly ancient group of reptiles. The oldest pterosaur fossils date back more than 200 million years. The first rhamphorhinchoid pterosaurs appeared about 180 million years ago. These long-tailed pterosaurs ruled the skies for nearly 80 million years before they died out about 100 million years ago. Long before that happened, however, one group of rhamphorhynchoids evolved into the short-tailed pterodactyloid pterosaurs. These animals eventually replaced the long-tails. The short-tailed pterosaurs survived until 65 million years ago, when a great **mass extinction** killed off both the short-tails and the dinosaurs.

At first glance, both types of pterosaur look pretty similar, except for the length of their tails. Close inspection of their fossil remains, however, shows that the rhamphorhynchoids and pterodactyloids were very different animals. In addition to their batlike front wings, the long-tails had a rear winglike membrane that connected the back legs to the tail. They also had long, sharp claws on their toes. These two features would have made walking and running on the ground very difficult. (Imagine trying to run while wearing long, pointed shoes with your legs wrapped in a tight-fitting cloth!)

Paleontologists believe that the long-tails behaved much like bats. When they weren't flying, they probably clambered on tree trunks, long-tailed **rhamphorhynchoid**. It's hard enough to believe that one type of pterosaur survived to modern times, let alone two.

People who believe the flying reptiles still exist aren't bothered by these arguments. After all, the story of the coelacanth proves that the fossil record doesn't always tell the whole story. If there are only a few pterosaurs in any

cliff faces, or cave walls until they found a resting place to hang from. The short-tails did not have that rear membrane, and they had short claws. This means they were probably good walkers and runners, but poor climbers. They may have rested on the ground, on cliff ledges, or on the floor of caves. Natives familiar with the behavior of the Kongamato and Ropen often claim that these beasts **roost** in caves. That is exactly where they would be expected to roost if they really were pterosaurs.

Almost all long-tails had sharp, needlelike teeth, which they used to snatch insects flying in the air or fish swimming near the surface of the water. Short-tails, by comparison, showed much more variety in their teeth. Some species had sharp teeth, just as the long-tails did, and probably ate the same types of food. Others had big crunching teeth that they used to crack snail and clam shells. A few had up to a thousand long, slender, closely spaced teeth that they used to strain tiny animals from the water. Some, such as the *Pteranodon*, had no teeth at all. They nabbed fish and shrimp with their long beaks, the way modern sea birds do.

It's interesting that so many pterosaurs were predators of animals that lived on, over, or under the water. That's where most Kongamato and Ropen sightings occur—either along coastlines or near rivers, lakes, and swamps.

The African saddle-billed stork sticks its legs straight out behind when it flies, making it look strikingly similar to a long-tailed pterosaur. This stork is probably responsible for many Kongamato sightings.

given area, and if they live mostly in remote places such as swamps and mountains, then it would be unlikely for people to find them or their remains very often. And if one of the two types of flying reptile had somehow managed to survive to the present, then why not the other type as well?

Such reasoning, however, does not persuade skeptical cryptozoologists. The Kongamato's reputation for breaking boats is particularly hard to accept. Pterosaurs could not fold their wings against their body the way diving birds do. So if an attacking pterosaur dove into the water like a pelican, its wings would take quite a beating. The long, skinny wing bones would probably snap in two, and the delicate wing membranes would be torn to shreds.

It's possible that the boat-breaker legend arose as a result of an actual attack by a large bird on a boat. Two birds capable of such an attack immediately come to mind. They are the saddle-billed stork (*Ephippiorhynchus senegalensis*) and the Marabou stork (*Leptotilos crumeniferus*). These big water birds are found over much of southern Africa, including many areas where the Kongamato has been sighted. The neck, head, and beak of both birds look similar to those of a pterosaur. In fact, at least one saddle-billed stork photograph has been mistakenly claimed as evidence for the existence of pterosaurs. These big birds stand nearly 5 feet tall (1.5 m) and have wingspans of 9 feet (2.7 m) or more. They can be frightful and dangerous at close range.

These storks construct big nests in trees near water. If a canoe approaches too closely to a stork's nest, the angry bird is likely to attack. As the people on board move around to avoid the vicious thrusts of the bird's sharp beak, the boat might **capsize**. Flavored with an extra pinch of imagination and half a spoonful of exaggeration, the story of such an attack could easily morph into the "Legend of the Kongamato."

Another interesting feature of these big storks is their color. Their body and wings are black and white, the same colors as the big beast that Kosi saw flying in the skies over Namibia. It is easy to overestimate the size of unfamiliar animals, especially when they are seen at a distance. Therefore, it seems quite possible that Kosi's black-and-white beast was nothing more than an airborne stork of exaggerated size.

Fruit bats are also good candidates for pterosaur look-alikes. These bats are found in tropical regions of Africa, Asia, New Guinea, and Australia—the same places where the Kongamato and Ropen have been reported. These bats have a doglike face, which is why they are sometimes called

The Ropen is often described as having a doglike face. Fruit bats, sometimes called flying foxes, also have a doglike face and are probably responsible for many Ropen sightings.

flying foxes. Some species of fruit bat are quite large, having a wingspan of 3 to 4 feet (0.9 to 1.2 m). This size wingspan is frequently reported in descriptions of modern-day pterosaurs, especially the Ropen.

While many, if not most, pterosaur reports are hoaxes or sightings of misidentified storks and fruit bats, some of them remain unexplained. In some places where pterosaurs have been reported, especially in some remote parts of Africa, the climate has changed little over the past 65 million years. If pterosaurs survived to the present day, they would have done so in places such as these, where time seems to stand still. Until a specimen of one is obtained, however, the Kongamato and Ropen must remain within the ranks of unknown animals.

Ri: Mermaid
From the
South Pacific

$\mathcal{N}$ ew Guinea is a hot spot for cryptid sightings. Pterosaurs and *Megalania*-sized lizards have each been reported there, and along the coast of one island a short distance east of New Guinea, an even more remarkable cryptid has been reported. That creature is a mermaid. For many generations, the natives of the island of New Ireland have claimed that a humanlike creature with fins lives in the ocean waters just offshore. It is called the Ri (pronounced "ree"). In 1979, the Ri caught the attention of American **anthropologist** Roy Wagner when he went to New Ireland to study the culture of the natives who lived there.

The Ri is said to live in the shallow water surrounding the island of New Ireland.

According to local legend, Ri are the spirits of a group of dancers who performed very poorly at an important ceremony. To make up for their poor performance, the dancers committed suicide by jumping off a cliff into the ocean. Their bodies became rocks along the shore, and their souls became Ri.

While talking to the natives, Wagner learned that one old man had come across a dead Ri when he was a child. The creature had apparently died in the water and washed up on the beach. Another man said that he often spotted Ri from his house near the shore. The man offered to take Wagner there, and Wagner accepted the invitation. Within a half an hour of Wagner's arrival at the house, his host saw a Ri in the distant shallows and excitedly pointed to it. Wagner saw the animal but did not get a clear view of it. He described it only as "a long dark body swimming at the surface horizontally."

LET'S GET TECHNICAL: DUGONGS

Dugongs are members of a group of aquatic mammals known as **sirenians**. Although there were once several species of sirenian, only four species have survived to modern times. Three of them are species of manatee, including the popular Florida manatee (*Trichechus manatus*), and the fourth is the dugong (*Dugong dugon*).

The dugong, a relative of the manatee, inhabits warm coastal waters of the Pacific and Indian oceans. It is common near the shores of New Ireland.

The Ri submerged and swam away when a nearby fish made a big splash in the water.

One islander told Wagner that when he was out in his fishing boat he had once come within 20 feet (6.1 m) of a Ri. He said the animal had the face of a monkey. Another man

---

The dugong's closest relative was the whale-sized Steller's sea cow (*Hydrodamalis gigas*). This animal inhabited the frigid waters of the northwestern Pacific Ocean until it was hunted to extinction in 1768. This was only 27 years after the species was discovered.

The dugong is found in tropical coastal waters of the Indian and Pacific Oceans. One of the largest populations of dugongs lives in the Torres Strait. This narrow strip of ocean passes between northern Australia and the southern coast of New Guinea. The Torres Strait is just 800 miles (1,280 km) southwest of New Ireland, the home of the Ri.

The dugong is easily identified by its tail. It has **flukes** like a whale's tale and looks nothing like the paddle-shaped tail of the manatee. It can reach 9 feet (2.7 m) in length and weigh up to 660 pounds (300 kg). It has smooth skin and a body that looks like a big, fat sausage. Its front flippers are shaped like paddles and it has the face of a walrus, without the tusks.

It might seem impossible that such an animal could be mistaken for a mermaid, but European sailors of long ago made that error. Sometimes this was a costly mistake. By chasing a "mermaid" as it swam in the shallow water, a ship could easily be torn apart by rocks and coral hidden below the surface. Such a mistake may be explained by the fact that the front end of a sirenian, when viewed from above the waves of the ocean surface, looks somewhat like a woman with a head of long, flowing hair.

had seen a male and female mating in the water. A young boy said he had seen three Ri one night—a male, a female, and a baby—swimming in a line near the mouth of a stream.

By talking with so many people, Wagner was able to put together a detailed description of the Ri's appearance and behavior. Its body from the waist up was very humanlike. It had long, dark hair and light-colored skin. It had hands with long fingernails. Female Ri had breasts like a woman. From the waist down, the Ri was more fishlike. Its legs were stuck together and, in place of feet, it had a pair of fins or flippers. The Ri was an air-breather, and it ate fish.

Wagner thought that the Ri must be some sort of mammal because it was an air breather and the females had breasts. He considered all the possibilities. He was sure that the islanders were not mistaking the Ri for the sea cow (a relative of the manatee). That animal was known to them. It had a separate name, *bo narasi*, which means "pig of the ocean." This was an important point to clarify. Sea cows, which are believed to have been the source of the mermaid legend in many other parts of the world, are known to inhabit the waters surrounding New Ireland. It's no coincidence that the sea cow's other name, *dugong*, means "lady of the sea."

Wagner was equally sure that the natives were not confusing the Ri with dolphins or porpoises. These speedy mammals sport a **dorsal fin** on their back, whereas the Ri had no dorsal fin and wasn't as fast a swimmer. Since seals and sea lions don't inhabit this part of the world, there seemed to be only one other possibility. The Ri was a creature unknown to modern science.

When Wagner returned to the United States, he contacted members of the International Society of Cryptozoology (ISC), an organization of cryptid hunters headquartered in Tucson, Arizona. Wagner told the ISC about the Ri. The ISC was intrigued by Wagner's report and decided to organize a Ri-hunting expedition.

When viewed from above, the outline of the front end of a dugong might be mistaken for a woman's head and body, giving rise to the belief in mermaids. In this photo, a woman dressed as a mermaid rests on a rock in the dugong exhibit at the Sydney Aquarium in Sydney, Australia.

THAR SHE BLOWS!

In the summer of 1983, Roy Wagner and ISC member Richard Greenwell arrived in New Ireland. They were there to lead a fact-finding expedition to try to solve the mystery of the Ri. One July morning, an animal was spotted near the surface of the water some distance offshore. It broke the surface of the water every 10 minutes, gulped fresh air, and then submerged. Two of the expedition members chased after the animal in a small boat. They managed to get within 50 feet (15.2 m) of it before it submerged one last time and disappeared. Two photographs of this animal were taken. Unfortunately, both were blurry and provided no clue as to the identity of the animal.

The investigators did obtain two bits of evidence that supported Wagner's belief that the Ri was not a dugong. The first one involved a 1978 scientific study of dugongs living off the coast of Australia. The study had shown that dugongs surface once a minute to breathe, whereas the Ri surfaced only once every 10 minutes. The second piece of evidence was that the Ri was a fairly fast swimmer. It seemed to be chasing fish—presumably to catch and eat them. By comparison, dugongs are slow swimmers and they are strict herbivores. Dugongs never eat fish.

With this limited information, the ISC investigators were unable to identify the Ri. In their official report in the journal *Cryptozoology*, however, the disappointed cryptozoologists ended their story on a positive note: "We are therefore left with the tantalizing possibility that the animal we observed is indeed new to science."

Mystery Solved

Finally, in 1985, the mystery of the Ri was solved during a high-tech expedition led by Thomas Williams of the Ecosophical Research Association (ERA). This organization investigates the source of legendary creatures such as the mermaid. Williams's team brought along a powerful motorboat to chase down any Ri that were spotted. The boat was equipped with underwater cameras and scuba gear, in case investigators got close enough to swim with a Ri and take its picture.

One afternoon, an animal was spotted as it waved its brown flukes in the air. According to Williams, the flukes looked like those of a whale. A native helper confirmed that the animal was a Ri. As was observed in the earlier expeditions, the Ri would submerge for approximately 10 minutes and then come up for a breath of fresh air.

One of the ERA investigators put on scuba gear and jumped into the water to get underwater photos of the animal. He estimated its length at about 5 feet (1.5 m). Its head was clearly visible, but it seemed to have no neck. The Ri had front limbs shaped like paddles. Its body was smooth and streamlined and ended with the tail that had been seen waving in the air above the surface. The Ri gracefully waved its flukes up and down as it slowly swam by. The diver said the animal looked like a dugong.

Another Ri was observed two days later, and divers were able to obtain crisp, clear underwater photos of the animal. They said the animal looked very much like a dugong. When they investigated the sea bottom where the Ri had been poking around with its snout, they found underwater plants growing in the sand. The Ri was apparently an herbivore, not a fish eater. As the evidence piled up, the Ri looked more and more like a dugong.

The expedition ended tragically on the fifth day. That morning, villagers pulled the dead body of a Ri out of the water. Close examination of the animal revealed a bullet hole in the animal's chest, near its right flipper. The animal's mouth was filled with water plants. The Ri had been shot to death while it was eating, perhaps when it surfaced for a breath of fresh air. With the dead Ri laid out on the beach for all to see, there was no longer any doubt—the Ri was a dugong.

Another Puzzle or Two

Although the identity of the Ri was finally determined, a couple of questions remained unanswered. First, why was the breathing pattern of the Ri so different from the one previously observed by scientists? As it turns out, the earlier study was done in very shallow water. The Ri observed in New Ireland, however, were feeding in water 50 feet (15.2 m) deep. This seems to indicate that dugongs stay submerged longer when they dive in deep water.

The second puzzle, and perhaps the greatest mystery of all, is how the villagers seem to view the dugong as both the Ri and the "pig of the ocean." The answer to this puzzle may have something to do with the way the natives of New Ireland view the world around them. For the modern-day scientist, the natural world is clearly separate from the supernatural world. For the people of New Ireland, however, the world is viewed as a combination of the natural and the supernatural. It's an ancient, fascinating, totally different way of thinking. It may be hard to understand, but with the help of anthropologists such as Wagner, someday it may start to make sense.

Final Report on the Giant Anaconda and Other Cryptids

*W*e've just trotted the globe in search of several unknown animals. Much has been learned about all of them, and the identity of one or two have been revealed. It is now time to summarize the findings and wrap up the investigation.

South America is home to one of the biggest snakes in the world, the green anaconda (*Eunectes murinus*). It is known to grow to a length of about 30 feet (9.1 m). But there are many reports of an even bigger snake, the *Sucuriju Gigante*, living in the Amazon rain forest. The Sucuriju supposedly grows to 50 feet (15.2 m) or more. While this monster may just be a jumbo green anaconda, some people believe that it could be a species unknown to science.

However, the case for the existence of the *Sucuriju Gigante* doesn't look good. No specimen of such a gigantic snake has ever come to light. A single jawbone from a dead Sucuriju would be enough evidence to confirm its existence, but the only evidence that supports the existence of the big snake comes in the form of stories and a carefully crafted photo of a dead and bloated, but not unusually large, green anaconda.

As Hyatt Verrill showed with his little experiment on estimating snake length, people tend to overestimate the length of snakes. Sometimes the exaggeration is as much as two or three times the snake's actual length. Taking this "Verrill effect" into account, it looks as though the *Sucuriju Gigante* may be nothing more than a 25- to 30-foot-long (7.6- to 9.1-m) anaconda. Still, until every nook and cranny of the vast Amazon rain forest is explored, we won't know for sure.

In the meantime, as global warming heats up the rain forest, green anacondas may grow larger, perhaps one day rivaling the extinct, 42.6-foot (13-m) *Titanoboa* in size. If this happens, the story of the *Sucuriju Gigante* will no longer be a just a legend.

The Chupacabras is an even more unlikely beast. The evidence shows that victims of the goatsucker were killed by dogs or coyotes. The few dead Chupacabras that have been examined by experts have turned out to be nothing more than mangy canines. The weird chimera type of Chupacabras commonly reported in Puerto Rico is most easily explained as a hoax. The other likely explanation is that the sightings are the product of overactive imaginations suffering from collective delusions or mass hysteria.

The giant squid was the source of the legend of the Kraken, a boat-sinking monster that haunted the world's oceans. Cryptozoologists believe that many of the unusual beasts described in legends and myths are actually real animals still unknown to science. This giant squid washed up on a beach in Tasmania in July 2007.

The two Australian cryptids considered in this investigation are both known animals that most scientists think are extinct. The fossil record indicates that the giant lizard *Megalania* has been gone for thousands of years. The last thylacines apparently vanished from the island of Tasmania in the mid-1900s. Yet sightings of both of these animals surface from time to time.

At least some *Megalania* sightings are probably explained by the Verrill effect. For example, in an eyewitness's mind, an 8-foot-tall (2.4 m) perentie lizard morphs into a 16-foot-tall (4.9-m) *Megalania*. Whether all such sightings can be explained this way remains to be seen. If *Megalania* can reproduce by means of parthenogenesis, then there's a remote possibility that this species exists in small, widely scattered populations in the vast Australian outback.

Because the Tasmanian wolf disappeared so recently, this animal would be one of the more likely cryptids to turn up in the flesh, especially on Tasmania. There are, however, lots of feral dogs, dingoes, and other canines roaming the island. These animals could easily be mistaken for a thylacine, especially from a long distance. Perhaps the only hope for the return of the Tasmanian wolf lies with the thylacine cloning project. That's a long shot at best.

Most cryptids live in remote, uninhabited areas such as mountains, swamps, or the deep ocean. The Thunderbird, however, is often sighted near towns and cities. Numerous sightings indicate that this huge raptor behaves just as a raptor should behave. It migrates between breeding and wintering grounds every year. This suggests to some cryptozoologists that the Thunderbird is real, not some imaginary beast. However, it also suggests that the Thunderbird is just a misidentified raptor, such as a golden eagle or an immature bald eagle, that morphs—courtesy of the Verrill effect—into a larger-than-life monster.

The scientific world was shocked when a live coelacanth was found off the coast of eastern Africa in 1938 because the fossil record indicated that the fish had been extinct for millions of years. Crypto-zoologists believe that other animals whose fossil record ended in the distant past (such as *Megalania*, teratorns, and pterosaurs) may still exist. This coelacanth was caught by Kenyan fisherman in 2001.

The Marlon Lowe story makes for fascinating reading, but without any solid evidence to back it up, it can hardly be considered as proof of the existence of an unknown species of condor-sized raptor. John Huffer's movie clip of the big bird of prey at Lake Shelbyville is the strongest evidence. It shows a very large raptor of some sort flying the skies of central Illinois a few days after the Lowe incident. Unfortunately, the bird in the movie can't be identified. It's possible that it's an unknown species. It's also possible that it's just a big specimen of a known species of vulture or eagle. Thus, for the present, the identity of the Thunderbird remains a mystery.

The possible existence of Kongamatos and Ropens is certainly exciting, but the evidence is weak. Any report about a flying reptile has to be taken with a big grain of salt, as there are known animals (such as fruit bats and storks) that could easily be mistaken for pterosaurs. The impossible boat-breaking behavior of the Kongamato is pretty good evidence that this animal is something other than a pterosaur. Possibly it is a nest-defending stork. If pterosaurs still exist, however, the timeless remote jungles in certain parts of Africa are where we would most likely find them. Someday, perhaps someone will.

The story of the Ri is a good example of what it takes to succeed in cryptozoology—**perseverance**. Anthropologist Roy Wagner gathered the first bits of information about the Ri by talking to the New Ireland natives. He then became involved in a cryptozoological investigation that gathered more information about the Ri. The animal was sighted again, but not long enough to be identified. It wasn't until a second expedition was launched that the Ri was finally identified as the dugong.

The fact that the Ri turned out to be an animal already known to science did not make the investigation a failure. On the contrary, it was a complete success. Cryptozoologists identified the unknown animal and solved the mystery of the New Ireland mermaid: The case was then closed.

LOWERING THE BAR

It is very difficult to obtain the type of evidence scientists demand before they are willing to accept the existence of a cryptid. Evidence such as actual body parts or even a complete specimen is required. That's why some cryptid hunters think the rules of cryptozoology should be changed. Just as you can lower the bar for the high jump so that it's easier to jump over, these people want to lower the bar for "proving" that a cryptid exists. They argue that a specimen isn't necessary if you can collect enough reports from honest eyewitnesses.

Following these simpler rules, some cryptid hunters say the Marlon Lowe incident is a very strong argument for the existence of Thunderbirds. Why? Because it fit so well with many other reports, which, if taken together, strongly suggested that an actual migration of giant raptors was under way in July of 1977. This explanation makes so much sense, it is argued, that no other explanation is needed.

The problem with this arguement is that it ignores the two possibilities that cryptozoologists always have to consider, especially when dealing with reports that are not backed up by an actual specimen. Those possibilities are hoaxes and cases of mistaken identity. That's precisely the problem with the Marlon Lowe incident. With only the story as evidence, it's impossible to determine whether the story was a hoax. In fact, the **credibility** of the Lowes' story was dealt a blow in 2007 when, in an episode of History Channel's *Monsterquest* TV show, the Lowes claimed that Marlon's attacker had a teratorn-sized 15-foot-wide (4.6-m) wingspan and a body as big as a man's—a bird almost twice the size of the bird they described in 1977! Even if the incident did occur, there's no way to determine whether Marlon's attacker was just a big raptor already known to science or whether it was some unknown monster bird.

You can't lower the bar in cryptozoology. You have to find a specimen of a cryptid to prove that it exists. That's always the hardest part of any cryptozoological investigation. Fortunately, many cryptozoologists enjoy the hunt for

In the 1800s, Europeans heard many stories from African pygmies about the okapi, a strange jungle animal that was half zebra and half giraffe. A British explorer finally discovered the okapi deep in the African rainforest in 1901. Cryptozoologists believe that many cryptids remain to be discovered in remote areas around the world.

the specimen. It's what makes the investigation so exciting, and the final results so satisfying.

ONE FINAL THOUGHT

Unknown animals come in all sorts of shapes, sizes, and colors. They fly or glide through the air; they walk, hop, or slither on the ground; or they swim through the water. Yet, they all have one thing in common—they play a good game of hide-and-seek. Even though cryptids have been encountered thousands of times, they rarely hang around long enough for anyone to determine their true identity. Cryptozoologists, however, sometimes get a lucky break and are able to turn an unknown animal into a known one.

Because cryptozoological investigations are rarely successful, some people think they are a waste of time and money. Other people think that these investigations are worth every second and every penny spent on them, because the discovery of any cryptid—a giant snake, a flying reptile, or a long-lost marsupial—could easily become the scientific find of the century. Both of these opinions make a good point, and people are sure to discuss this issue for a long time to come. What do you think?

GLOSSARY

Aborigines   Australia's first human inhabitants, who came there from Asia 50,000 years ago

Anaconda   A large South American snake that kills its prey by squeezing it in its coils

Anatomy   The structure of an organism

Anthropologist   A person who studies the customs, culture, or fossil remains of human beings

Arachnid   A type of animal that has eight legs (for example, spiders, mites, and ticks)

Bacteria   A type of microscopic, single-celled organism; some bacteria decompose dead plants and animals.

Binomial nomenclature   A two-part naming system for living things, consisting of the genus and species names

Bloated   Swollen or puffed up

Bounty   A reward given for the killing or capture of an animal

Canine   Any type of dog (for example, the wolf, fox, and coyote)

Capsize   To turn over or turn bottom side up

Carrion   Dead, decaying flesh

Cast   An object shaped in a mold; a footprint cast is made by pouring liquid plaster into the footprint, and then removing the plaster in one piece after it has hardened.

Chimera   An animal made from the body parts of different kinds of animals

Climate change   A change in the type of weather a place has year after year

Clone   The verb form means to produce an animal from the DNA of one of the body cells of another animal. A clone (noun) is an exact copy of the other animal, since it has the same DNA.

Coelacanth   A large fish from the Indian Ocean, thought to have been extinct for several million years until a live specimen was caught in 1938

Collective delusion   An emotional, chain-reaction-type of response among people in a group

Constrictor   A snake that kills its prey by squeezing it in its coils

Corroborate   To back up, confirm, or support

Credibility   The state of being believable or reliable

Cryptid   An unknown animal that some people believe exists, even though there is not enough evidence to prove its existence

Cryptozoology   The study of unknown animals

Decompose   To rot or decay

Dehydrated   Dried out

DNA (Deoxyribonucleic acid)   The substance that genes are made from

Domesticated   Changed from a wild to a tame state

Dorsal fin   A fin that sticks up on the back of fishes and whales

Extinct   No longer in existence

Feral   Gone back to the original wild condition after having been domesticated

Fluke   Either of the two halves of a whale's tail

Flyway   A route followed by migrating birds

Fossil   A preserved body part or traces of a once-living thing

Genus   A group of closely related species

Gland   An organ of the body that releases a substance into or out of the body (for example, a venom gland or a sweat gland)

Global warming   Warming of Earth's climate as a result of a buildup of greenhouse gases (especially carbon dioxide) that trap heat radiating from the planet's surface

Habitat   The place where a living thing normally lives (for example, a rain forest or a desert).

Herbivore   An animal that feeds mainly on plants

Herpetologist   A scientist who studies reptiles and amphibians

Host   A living thing on or in which a parasite lives

Humanoid   Having human characteristics

Hybrid   The offspring of a male and a female of different species

Immature   Young, not an adult

Loins   The part of an animal's body between the ribs and the hips

Mange   Skin disease caused by parasitic mites

Marsupial   A mammal that carries its young in a pouch (for example, a kangaroo)

Mass extinction   A situation in which many types of living things become extinct within a relatively short period of time

Mass hysteria   A situation in which a whole group of people feels similar symptoms of illness, such as headaches and dizziness

Mite   A tiny arachnid parasite that lives on an animal's skin

Migrate   To move from one place to another with the change in the seasons

Mutilation   A condition in which an animal's body is beaten up or severely injured, often resulting in its death

Nocturnal   Active during the night

Outback   Australian wilderness areas far away from cities and towns

Paleontologist   A scientist who studies ancient life-forms

Parasite   An animal that lives on or in another animal from which it gets its food

Parthenogenesis   A type of reproduction in which a female produces young without breeding with a male

Penal colony   A prison located in a faraway place, often on a remote island, where escape is almost impossible

Perseverance   Not quitting or giving up

Poikilothermic   Having a body temperature that varies with the environmental temperature; cold-blooded

Ponderous   Very big and heavy

Population   All the members of a single species living in one place

Predator   An animal that eats other animals

Pterodactyloid   One of two types of prehistoric flying reptile, characterized by a short tail

Pterosaur   A prehistoric flying reptile

Python   A large snake from Africa, Asia, or Australia that kills its prey by squeezing it in its coils

Raptor   A bird of prey (for example, an eagle or hawk)

Relict   Surviving from an earlier time

Rhamphorhynchoids   One of two types of prehistoric flying reptile, characterized by a long tail

Roost   Rest for the night

Scale   A comparison of the size of two objects. If the size of one of the objects is known, the size of the other object can be determined from it.

Scapegoat   A person or animal picked to bear the blame for someone else's mistake

Serrated   Toothed or notched, like the edge of a saw blade

Sirenian   A manatee or dugong, also known as a "sea cow"

Skeptical   Tending to doubt

Species   A single type of plant or animal, such as the green anaconda. Closely related species are grouped together into a genus.

Specimen   An example of a plant, animal, or mineral

Surrogate   A substitute or replacement

Talon   The claw of a bird of prey

Taxidermist   A person who prepares, stuffs, and mounts animal skins so the animals look alive

Teratorn   A gigantic, extinct bird of prey related to vultures

Uterus   The part of a female mammal's body that holds and feeds the young before birth; the womb

Venomous   Poisonous

Vertebrae   The bones that form the backbone

BIBLIOGRAPHY

BOOKS, PERIODICALS, AND VIDEOS

Coleman, Loren, and Jerome Clark. *Cryptozoology A to Z: The Encyclopedia of Loch Ness Monsters, Sasquatch, Chupacabras, and Other Authentic Mysteries of Nature.* New York: Simon and Schuster, 1999.

Corrales, Scott. *Chupacabras and Other Mysteries.* Murphreesboro, Tenn.: Greenleaf Publications, 1997.

Dinsdale, Tim. *Monster Hunt.* Washington, D.C.: Acropolis Books, 1972.

Edmonds, Marge, and E.E. Clark. *Voices of the Winds: Native American Legends.* New York: Facts on File, 1989.

Hall, Mark A. *Thunderbirds: America's Living Legends of Giant Birds.* New York: Paraview Press, 2004.

Head, Jason J., et al. "Giant Boid Snake from the Palaeocene Neotropics Reveals Hotter Past Equatorial Temperatures." *Nature.* 457 (2009): 715–717.

Mittelbach, Margaret, and M. Crewdson. *Carnivorous Nights: On the Trail of the Tasmanian Tiger.* New York: Villard Books, 2005.

Monterquest: The Complete Season One. A&E Television Network. Distributed by New Video. ©2007, 2008.

Murphy, John C., and R.W. Henderson. *Tales of Giant Snakes: A Historical Natural History of Anacondas and Pythons.* Malabar, Fla.: Krieger Publishing, 1997.

Nickell, Joe. *The Mystery Chronicles: More Real-Life X-Files.* Lexington: The University Press of Kentucky, 2004.

Owen, David. *Tasmanian Tiger: The Tragic Tale of How the World Lost its Most Mysterious Predator.* Baltimore: Johns Hopkins University Press, 2003.

Paddle, Robert. *The Last Tasmanian Tiger: The History and Extinction of the Thylacine.* Cambridge: Cambridge University Press, 2000.

Peterson, Roger Tory. *A Field Guide to the Birds*. Boston: Houghton Mifflin, 1947.

Pope, Clifford H. *The Giant Snakes: The Natural History of the Boa Constrictor, the Anaconda, and the Largest Pythons*. New York: Alfred A. Knopf, 1980.

Radford, Benjamiin. "Latest Texas 'Chupacabra' Exibited in Creationist Museum." *Skeptical Inquirer* 34, no. 1 (1009):7.

Shuker, Karl P.N. *In Search of Prehistoric Survivors: Do Giant "Extinct" Creatures Still Exist?* London: Blandford, 1995.

Unwin, David M. *The Pterosaurs From Deep Time*. New York: Pi Press, 2006.

Wagner, Roy. "The Ri: Unidentified Aquatic Animals of New Ireland, Papua New Guinea." *Cryptozoology* 1 (1982): 33–39.

Wagner, Roy, J.R. Greenwell, G.J. Raymond, and K. Von Nieda. "Further Investigations Into the Biological and Cultural Affinities of the Ri." *Cryptozoology* 2 (1983): 113–125.

Wells, H.G. *The Island of Dr. Moreau*. New York: Bantam Books, 1994.

Williams, Thomas R. "Identification of the Ri Through Further Fieldwork in New Ireland, Papua New Guinea." *Cryptozoology* 4 (1985): 61–68.

WEB SITES

"2007 Autumn HawkWatch." HawkMountain.org. Available online. URL: http://data.hawkmountain.org/cgi-bin/count/viewdateframe-year2008.cgi. Accessed October 5, 2009.

Audubon, John James. "Washington Sea Eagle." Audobon.org. Available online. URL: http://www.audubon.org/bird/BoA/F2_G4a.html. Accessed October 5, 2009.

Bartholomew, Robert E., and E. Goode. "Mass Delusions and Hysterias: Highlights from the Past Millennium." Committee for the Scientific Investigation of Claims of the Paranormal. Available online. URL: http://www.csicop.org/si/2000-05/delusions.html. Accessed October 5, 2009.

Carroll, Robert Todd. "Chupacabra." Skeptic's Dictionary. Available online. URL: http://skepdic.com/chupa.html. Accessed October 5, 2009.

Ciofi, Claudio. "The Komodo Dragon." Scientific American, March 1999. Available online. URL: http://www.sciam.com/article.cfm?id=the-komodo-dragon. Accessed October 5, 2009.

"Climate Change Caused Extinction of Australia's Giant Animals." Environment News Service, June 1, 2005. Available online. URL: http://www.ens-newswire.com/ens/jun2005/2005-06-01-02.asp. Accessed October 5, 2009.

Fry, Bryan G., et al. "Early Evolution of the Venom System in Lizards and Snakes." *Nature*. 439, February 2006: 584–588. Available online. URL: http://www.venomdoc.com/downloads/2005_BGF_Nature_squamate_venom.pdf. Accessed October 5, 2009.

"Golden Eagle." Oregon Zoo Animals. Available online. URL: http://www.oregonzoo.org/Cards/BirdsOfPrey/golden_eagle.htm. Accessed October 5, 2009.

"Greyhound Racing Tracks in Australia." AussieSportsinfo.com. Available online. URL: http://www.aussiesportsinfo.com/greyhounds/. Accessed October 5, 2009.

Koehler, P.G. "Mange." University of Florida IFAS Extension. Available online. URL: http://edis.ifas.ufl.edu/mg118. Accessed October 5, 2009.

Pierce, Tony. "Is That a Chupacabra Being Stuffed by a Taxidermist in Texas?" *Los Angeles Times*. September 2, 2009. Available online. URL: http://latimesblogs.latimes.com/unleashed/2009/09/chupacabra-found-and-stuffed-by-taxidermist-in-texas.html. Accessed December 11, 2009.

"Zoo Celebrates Virgin Birth of Komodo Dragons." MSNBC.com, January 25, 2007. Available online. URL: http://www.msnbc.msn.com/id/16784022. Accessed October 5, 2009.

FURTHER RESOURCES

Arment, Chad. *Cryptozoology: Science and Speculation*. Landisville, Penn.: Coachwhip Publications, 2004.

Coghlan, Ronan. *A Dictionary of Cryptozoology*. New York: Excalibur Publishing, 2004.

Coleman, Loren, and J. Clark. *Cryptozoology A-Z: The Encyclopedia of Loch Monsters, Sasquatch, Chupacabras, and Other Authentic Mysteries of Nature*. New York: Fireside Books, 1999.

Holmes, Thom, and L. Holmes. *Prehistoric Flying Reptiles: the Pterosaurs*. Berkeley Heights, N.J.: Enslow Publishers, 2003.

Martin, James. *Komodo Dragons: Giant Lizards of Indonesia*. Mankato, Minn.: Capstone Press, 1995.

Newton, Michael. *Encyclopedia of Cryptozoology: A Global Guide to Hidden Animals and Their Pursuers*. Jefferson, N.C.: McFarland, 2005.

O'Neill, Terry. *The Chupacabras*. Farmington Hills, Mich.: KidHaven Press, 2007.

Shuker, Karl P.N. *The Beasts that Hide From Man: Seeking the World's Last Undiscovered Animals*. New York: Paraview Press, 2003.

WEB SITES

Cryptomundo.com
http://www.cryptomundo.com/
A cryptozoology Web site with links to Web pages about many of the most popular cryptids. Also reports on news stories, meetings, and conferences about cryptids.

Cryptozoology.com
http://www.cryptozoology.com/
A cryptozoology Web site with detailed descriptions of many cryptids. Also has a list of cryptid sightings and a photo gallery of unidentified animals.

Cryptozoology: The Study of Unknown Animals
http://kodos86.tripod.com/cryptozoology/index.html
A cryptozoology Web site with information about almost
every cryptid included in the Creature Scene Investigation series.
Also has a section on "Frequently Asked Questions" about
cryptozoology.

ExtremeScience.com
http://www.extremescience.com/BiggestSnake.htm
A Web site describing the green anaconda. Includes a link to a
story about a herpetologist who studies anacondas in the wild.

Thylacine Museum
http://www.naturalworlds.org/thylacine/
Contains everything you want to know about the thylacine.
Includes actual black-and-white movie clips of the last remaining
thylacines living at the Hobart Zoo in Tasmania.

PICTURE CREDITS

INDEX

ABOUT THE AUTHOR

RICK EMMER is a substitute science and math teacher for the Avon Lake City School District in northeast Ohio. He was previously an aquarist at the Cleveland Aquarium and a zookeeper at the Cleveland Metroparks Zoo. He has a bachelor's degree in biology from Mount Union College and a master's degree in biology from John Carroll University. He was a member of the International Society of Cryptozoology for several years. Emmer lives with his family in Bay Village, Ohio, smack dab in the middle of Cryptid Country, with the lair of the Lake Erie Monster to the north and the hideout of the Grassman, Ohio's Bigfoot, to the south.